# Deadly Dogma:

## How Neoconservatives
## Broke the Law to Deceive America

by

Grant F. Smith

An Institute for Research: Middle Eastern Policy,
Inc. (IRmep) Book

Published by the Institute for Research: Middle Eastern Policy
Calvert Station
PO Box 32041
Washington, DC 20007

http://www.IRmep.org

First published in 2006 by the Institute for Research: Middle
Eastern Policy

7   9   10   8   6

Library of Congress Cataloging-in-Publication Data

Smith, Grant F.
Deadly dogma : how neoconservatives broke the law to
deceive America / by Grant F. Smith.
p. cm.
Includes bibliographical references.
ISBN 0-9764437-4-0 (alk. paper)
1. Conservatism--United States. 2. Law--Political aspects--
United States. 3. United States--Foreign relations--2001- 4.
United States--Politics and government--2001- I. Title.
JC573.2.U6S643 2006
973.931--dc22

2006007082

*Choose your leaders with wisdom and forethought. To be led by a coward is to be controlled by all that the coward fears.*

*To be led by a fool is to be led by the opportunists who control the fool.*

*To be led by a thief is to offer up your most precious treasures to be stolen.*

*To be led by a liar is to ask to be lied to.*

*To be led by a tyrant is to sell yourself and those you love into slavery.*

\*\*\*

*Beware, all too often we say what we hear others say.*

*We think what we are told that we think.*

*We see what we are permitted to see.*

*Worse, we see what we are told that we see.*

*Repetition and pride are the keys to this.*

*To hear and to see even an obvious lie again and again and again, maybe to say it almost by reflex, and then to defend it because we have said it, and at last to embrace it because we've defended it.*

**Octavia Butler**

# Table of Contents

Table of Figures and Legal References ................................. 12
About the Author ....................................................................... 15
Prologue: .................................................................................... 16
What Is a Neocon? ..................................................................... 19
   Neoconservative Objectives ................................................. 23
Dogma #1: Strike "First" ......................................................... 25
   Wolfowitz and First Strike Theory ..................................... 25
   First-Strike Mythology and the 1967 Six-Day War .......... 29
   The Hidden Benefits of First-Strike Doctrine .................... 36
   Occupying Ill-Gotten Territory ............................................ 38
Dogma #2: Unlimited Military Spending ................................ 41
   A New Century of Unwarranted Spending ......................... 42
   Frank Gaffney and the Domino's Pizza of Policy ............. 48
   Military Contracts: A New Protection Racket ................... 53
   The Boeing Tanker Leasing Deal ....................................... 55
   The Cost of Neocon Intermediation .................................... 59
Dogma #3: The Nobility of Lies .............................................. 63
   From Leo Strauss to the Great WMD Hoax of 2002 ........ 67
   The Consequences of Noble Lies ........................................ 74
Dogma #4: Plunder and Saturate Media Networks ................. 77
   Payola for Pundits ............................................................... 80
   America's Largest Privately Subsidized "News" Sources 84
Dogma #5: The Primacy of Israel ............................................ 87
   Neocon Membership Requirements ..................................... 99
   Stifling Debate .................................................................. 100
   Means Versus Ends ............................................................ 101
Dogma #6: International Law Is Non-Binding ..................... 105
   Canceling the Chemical Weapons Convention for Profit 109
   International Extortion ....................................................... 110
   Charitable Lawbreaking ..................................................... 112
   Overseas Charitable Laundering, Fraud, and Ethnic
   Cleansing ........................................................................... 115
   US Nonprofit Involvement in Illegal Settlement
   Coordination ...................................................................... 120
   The Legal Dilemmas of Israel and Terrorism .................. 122
   Consequences of Lawbreaking .......................................... 123
Neocons: America's New Mafia? ........................................... 125
   Evolving Prosecutorial Climate ........................................ 126

Espionage ................................................................ 128
Conspiracy and Wire Fraud ...................................... 135
Military Contract Fraud .......................................... 138
Private Correspondence with Foreign Governments ....... 139
Extortion ............................................................... 140
Military Expeditions Against a Friendly Nation ............ 142
Filing False Tax Returns and Charity Fraud ................. 145
Bribery of Public Officials and Conflicts of Interest ...... 146
The Larger Crime Syndicate ..................................... 151
Conclusions ............................................................ 156
Appendix A: PNAC Letter to Bill Clinton ..................... 159
Appendix B: Arab-Israeli Crisis and War, 1967 .............. 163
Appendix C: The Clean Break Plan .............................. 223
Appendix D: Gas Stations in the Sky ........................... 233
Appendix E: Adbusters ............................................. 237
End Notes .............................................................. 241

## Table of Figures and Legal References

Poll: Do you think the Bush administration deliberately misled
       the American public about whether Iraq has weapons of
       mass destruction, or not? ............................................ 71
Tax-Exempt Donation Laundering and Terrorism Against the
       US ...................................................................... 116
Tax-Exempt Donation Laundering for Beitar Illit Arms
       Purchases .............................................................. 118
US Tax-Exempt Donors to Illegal Settlements .................... 119
US Nonprofit Control of the World Zionist Organization
       Settlement Division .................................................. 121
A Short History of Neocon Espionage ............................. 131
USC 18 >PART I>CHAPTER 37>Espionage and Censorship
       ....................................................................... 134
USC 18>PART I >CHAPTER 19 >§ 371
       Conspiracy to commit offense or to defraud United
       States                                         ......... 137
USC 18 > PART I > CHAPTER 15 >  § 286. Conspiracy to
       defraud the Government with respect to claims ......... 138
USC 18 > PART I > CHAPTER 45 > § 953. Private
       correspondence with foreign governments ................. 139

USC 18 > PART I > CHAPTER 41 >§ 872. Extortion by officers or employees of the United States.................141

USC 18 > CHAPTER 45--FOREIGN RELATIONS > § 960 Expedition against friendly nation ..............................143

USC 18 > CHAPTER 45--FOREIGN RELATIONS > § 960 Expedition against friendly nation ..............................143

USC 18>CHAPTER 45--FOREIGN RELATIONS>§ 956 Conspiracy to kill, kidnap, maim, or injure persons or damage property in a foreign country .........................143

USC 26 > SUBTITLE F > CHAPTER 75 > Subchapter A > PART I § 7206. Fraud and false statements (2) Aid or assistance....................................................................145

USC 18 > PART I > CHAPTER 11 §201 Bribery of public officials and witnesses.................................................146

USC 18 > PART I > CHAPTER 11 > § 208 ........................150

Acts affecting a personal financial interest..........................150

La Cosa Nuovo – Leadership Structure and Duties.............154

# About the Author

Grant F. Smith is director of research at the Institute for Research: Middle Eastern Policy (IRmep), a Washington D.C.-based nonprofit organization. Smith's research and analysis have appeared in the Financial Times of London, Reuters, Arab News, Gannet, The Wall Street Journal, the New York Times, the Daily Star, the Associated Press, and specialty publications such as the US State Department's "Washington File." Smith has personally appeared on Voice of America (VOA) television, C-SPAN, and CNN.

Smith's research has taken him to more than forty countries, on assignments ranging from as little as a few days to a half-decade. Before joining IRmep, he was a senior analyst and later a program manager and consultant at the Boston-based Yankee Group Research, Inc., where he worked on investments of over $3 billion in development projects in thirty countries in conjunction with private corporations, investment banks, and NGOs.

Before that, he worked as a marketing manager at the Minneapolis-based Investors Diversified Services (IDS), now Ameriprise Financial Advisors. Smith's formal education includes a BA in International Relations from the University of Minnesota and a master's degree in International Management from the University of St. Thomas in St Paul, Minnesota. Smith's career in research includes the authorship of over 140 research papers, articles, and editorials on international issues.

# Prologue:

In the final semester of the 2005 academic year, the dean of Georgetown University's School of Foreign Service proposed hiring Douglas Feith as a visiting professor. The former undersecretary of defense for policy and Georgetown graduate had announced his early retirement from the Pentagon under suspicious circumstances in early 2005, a few months before damaging news hit the mainstream media. One of Feith's subordinates, Colonel Lawrence Franklin, pled guilty to passing classified Department of Defense information to an Israeli lobby as well as Israeli diplomats. A massive FBI investigation was still interviewing dozens of former officials in Feith's Pentagon "Office of Special Plans" to answer questions about the use of faulty intelligence to provide a pretext for the US invasion of Iraq. A separate Senate investigation was also underway.

That Feith should be offered a prestigious post at a top American foreign affairs college even before the smoke of controversy cleared is not particularly surprising. Many in the upper tiers of the Washington establishment either do not recognize or wish to obscure the extensive damage Feith and his neoconservative fellow travelers have visited upon the United States. The neocon masterpiece is the US invasion of Iraq, an unprecedented modern first strike and war of choice that has cost upwards of 100,000 Iraqi lives (half of them women and children).[1] According to the Department of Defense, over 2,262 American soldiers have been killed in Iraq. 16,653 have been wounded in action.[2] The cost of the invasion will approach $1.1 trillion, assuming a diminishing troop presence in Iraq over the next five years. This estimate may fall short if US bases now under construction become permanent. [3] Sold to the American public as a preemptive attack to protect America from Saddam Hussein's weapons of mass destruction, in reality the plans to invade Iraq had been carefully nurtured and pushed by neoconservatives over the course of decades. No other center of thinking, lobbying, and political power had as much influence in fomenting war as the neoconservatives.

Feith neither worked alone nor accomplished the first strike on Iraq and other damaging initiatives singlehandedly. The "neoconservative movement" of intellectuals, ideologues, and hucksters swimming in an inky nexus of politics, defense contract commissions, self-promotion, and mass media punditry is now fairly well documented. Their biographies and proclaimed worldview are well known; their talking points and ubiquitous policy analysis have long been all but unavoidable.

While many books have been written by neoconservatives lauding themselves, this book represents an outside attempt to compare neoconservative operations with dogma crafted for the outside world. Some parts of this dogma, such as the neocon mantra of unlimited military spending, are loudly and proudly marketed to the outside world. Others, such as the necessity of the "Noble Lie," are internal operating principles that the neocons often deny under the harsh light of outside scrutiny.

After close examination, most neoconservative principles can be said to be "authoritative without adequate grounds"—Merriam-Webster's definition of dogma. Since it has little inherent merit or value, promoters of neoconservative dogma have had to plunder corporations such as Hollinger International and tap the US treasury to secure funding and mass media distribution. Neoconservatives have relied on the largesse of military contractors and corrupt defense deals to provide huge sums of working capital for their causes. Through intimidation and smear tactics, they have erected a defensive gauntlet around themselves that few dare run.

The shallow sloganeering and weak central tenets of neoconservatism have many strong and prominent defenders. Those who challenge neoconservatives too vigorously, no matter what their politics are, have been smeared as "anti-Semites" or "traitors" by neoconservative media hit men.

***Deadly Dogma:***
***How Neoconservatives Broke the Law to Deceive America***

In the following chapters, we empirically analyze the results of the fatally flawed dogma at the core of neoconservatism. We attempt to quantify the opportunity cost of neocon policy while making a case that the neocon network's track record of criminality buttressed by cross-promotion is best compared to a new Mafia. We briefly discuss their documented history of lawbreaking and the appropriate law enforcement remedies that would shut down the latest crime syndicate to blight America.

# What Is a Neocon?

This book attempts to show the real essence of neoconservatism as it is practiced. Neoconservatives are best known for their words, not their deeds; this may be their best defense mechanism. The following chapters examine different aspects of neoconservative dogma from unique perspectives. However, it is constructive to first answer the question "What is a neocon?" starting with the definitions and statements put forth by self-identified members of the group, including Irwin Seltzer and Max Boot:

> "The Neocon position might be summed up as diplomacy if possible, force if necessary; the UN if possible, ad hoc coalitions or unilateral action if necessary; preemptive strikes if it is reasonable to anticipate hostile action on the part of America's enemies." **Irwin Seltzer[4]**

> Neocons are not 'soft Wilsonians', like former President Jimmy Carter, but are 'hard Wilsonians' who place their faith not in pieces of paper, but in power, specifically U.S. power.' **Max Boot, paraphrased by Irwin Seltzer[5]**

These definitions fall short on several counts. In the chapter **Dogma #1: Strike "First,"** we reveal how the so-called preemptive strike doctrine, while doing little to defend America from "hostile action," has concentrated power in the hands of neoconservatives while moving decision criteria into the realm of the subjective. In the chapter **Dogma #6: International Law is Non-Binding**, we examine how neoconservative scholars and activists make diplomacy, UN action, and non-governmental organization (NGO) irrelevant by systematically undermining international law.

It is disingenuous to consider neocon ideology to be "Wilsonian" in any way. Scholars of diplomacy often refer to President Wilson's "14 Points" speech delivered to Congress on January 8, 1918, outlining his steps for reconstructing Europe following World War I and moving toward creating a permanent peace. These points encapsulate the essence of Wilsonian ideals.

> "1. Open covenants of peace, openly arrived at, after which there shall be no private international understandings of any kind but diplomacy shall proceed always frankly and in the public view." **Woodrow Wilson, 1918**

In the chapter **Dogma #3: The Nobility of Lies**, we describe the neoconservative strategy of cloaking controversial policies in "Noble Lies" to deceive the American public. Wilson would no doubt be shocked and horrified at the "Downing Street Memos" showing the secret collusion of ostensibly colonial powers coordinating and distributing a public message of diplomacy to their citizens, even as imminent invasion and occupation plans were being implemented. The coordinated media campaign of "Noble Lies" intended to generate American support for the neocons' largest strategic objective, the invasion of Iraq, was remarkably un-Wilsonian. However, one should not stop with point one.

> "4. Adequate guarantees given and taken that national armaments will be reduced to the lowest point consistent with domestic safety." **Woodrow Wilson, 1918**

Arms control and reduction are anathema to neoconservatives, as we discuss in the chapter **Dogma #2: Unlimited Military**

**Spending**. Arms reduction and arms control would eliminate brokerage premiums needed to keep the neocon network alive. Neoconservatives such as Frank Gaffney, Richard Perle, and signatories of Project for the New American Century initiatives have an unbroken record of opposing arms control treaties while promoting even the most destabilizing weapons, such as chemical and biological agents, and advocating arms races in "new frontiers" like space. It is a cynical perversion of Wilson's legacy to describe neoconservatives as Wilsonian in matters concerning armaments and military power.

It is equally perverse to believe that neoconservatives are disciples of the principles of self-determination outlined in Wilson's point five.

> "5. A free, open-minded, and absolutely impartial adjustment of all colonial claims, based upon a strict observance of the principle that in determining all such questions of sovereignty the interests of the populations concerned must have equal weight with the equitable claims of the government whose title is to be determined. " **Woodrow Wilson, 1918**

One of the last significant colonial questions, that of the state of Israel, has enjoyed absolute US weight on the side of the Israelis, thanks in part to neocon thought leadership and lobbying, which is partisan to Israeli retention of occupied territories, nuclear weapons, and subsidies from the US. These terms are the exact opposite of what Wilson would have demanded as a just settlement for Palestinians. We discuss this in the chapter **Dogma #5: The Primacy of Israel**. Today, the Palestinian territories greatly resemble the German-occupied Belgium of Wilson's day. The fact that illegal Israeli settlements and brutal military occupations continue in violation of international law undermines world confidence in the rule of law.

> "7. Belgium, the whole world will agree, must be evacuated and restored, without any attempt to limit the sovereignty which she enjoys in common with all

> other free nations. No other single act will serve as this will serve to restore confidence among the nations in the laws which they have themselves set and determined for the government of their relations with one another. Without this healing act the whole structure and validity of international law is forever impaired." **Woodrow Wilson, 1918**

If Palestine is the world's modern-day Belgium, it enjoys none of the privileges from Wilson's point 14:

> "14. A general association of nations must be formed under specific covenants for the purpose of affording mutual guarantees of political independence and territorial integrity to great and small states alike." **Woodrow Wilson, 1918**

It is puzzling that prominent neoconservatives would claim that their movement and its accomplishments are in any way "Wilsonian." It is far more plausible that the peripheral policies rejecting the legitimacy of international law while relying upon the US military as the sole global authority actually serve the real core principle of neoconservatism: the primacy of Israel.

We find it more productive to craft a definition based on observable facts and behavior of members of the group. This in-depth review of the history and operations of the neocon network in America leads to a less fawning and wholly more accurate definition. We prefer this short definition encompassing the major components of the system, its observable objectives, and how it interacts with the world:

> "Neocons are individuals who are direct or indirect military contract profiteers who extort public insecurity for individual and collective wealth and power. Contemptuous of international and US law, they empower and promote a wider network of collaborators and militants to achieve predefined policy objectives and their own conception of Israeli

interests, which are then usually marketed as 'defending America.' "

# *Neoconservative Objectives*

Through observable actions and affiliations that are revealed in this book, neoconservatives have demonstrated their core objectives:

1.  Dominate US foreign policy making and definitions of "the enemy"

2.  Embed and perpetuate the neocon ideological network at the top levels of the US government

3.  Change, subvert, or ignore laws that impede "the cause"

4.  Advance and enforce an idealized conceptualization of Israel based on a selective historical memory

5.  Extort and otherwise obtain and spread wealth and resources sufficient to finance "the cause"

The pursuit of neoconservative objectives has led to a great many criminal acts by individual neoconservatives and the network as a whole. Although the analogy is not a perfect fit, it is most useful to think of the neocon network as a new kind of organized crime syndicate or Mafia. Like the Mafia, the network's goal is not breaking the law, but rather wealth, power, influence, and the capability to deceive on a massive scale; however, as the Mafia has also found, the quickest route to wealth, power, and influence involves systematic and premeditated lawbreaking.

Our final chapter, **Neocons, America's New Mafia,** examines the history of neoconservative lawbreaking from extortion and espionage to tax fraud, and makes the argument that the time has come for increased law enforcement actions.

# Dogma #1: Strike "First"

It is official military policy that the United States of America will deter challenges from rivals through limitless spending and military preemption. This relatively new and radical doctrine is the result of thirty years of behind-the-scenes neoconservative machinations. Preemption provides unlimited opportunities for neocon power-brokering of military spending (discussed in chapter 2), permanent political positioning on the "high" strategic rhetorical ground of "defending America," and opportunities to direct and channel American military might against Israeli rivals (discussed in chapter 5).

Preemption hasn't always been embedded in US military strategy. Its inclusion is the culmination of years of efforts by Paul Wolfowitz and a constellation of other neoconservative thinkers and cheerleaders to integrate the first-strike mentality into formal American defense strategy.

All the major spending elements of the preemptive national security strategy, including regime change in Iraq, "more usable" nuclear arms, denial of nuclear weapons to non-nuclear states, and deployment of exorbitantly expensive "Star Wars" missile intercept systems, were crafted and promoted by neoconservative think tanks such as the Project for the New American Century, the American Enterprise Institute, the Center for Security Policy, and the National Institute for Public Policy long before George W. Bush took office.

## *Wolfowitz and First Strike Theory*

In 2002, former Undersecretary of Defense Paul Wolfowitz presented a new and fundamentally radical strategy for defending the United States. His plan, titled "The National Security Strategy of the United States of America," is still the country's guiding strategic military document at the time of this writing.

A central strategy in the document is preemption, or striking at "gathering threats":

> "We must adapt the concept of imminent threat to the capabilities and objectives of today's adversaries. Rogue states and terrorists do not seek to attack us using conventional means. They know such attacks would fail. Instead, they rely on acts of terror and, potentially, the use of weapons of mass destruction—weapons that can be easily concealed, delivered covertly, and used without warning.
>
> The targets of these attacks are our military forces and our civilian population, in direct violation of one of the principal norms of the law of warfare. As was demonstrated by the losses on September 11, 2001, mass civilian casualties is the specific objective of terrorists and these losses would be exponentially more severe if terrorists acquired and used weapons of mass destruction. The United States has long maintained the option of preemptive actions to counter a sufficient threat to our national security. The greater the threat, the greater is the risk of inaction—and the more compelling the case for taking anticipatory action to defend ourselves, even if uncertainty remains as to the time and place of the enemy's attack. To forestall or prevent such hostile acts by our adversaries, the United States will, if necessary, act preemptively." **National Security Strategy of the United States of America** [6]

Wolfowitz began his road to preemption as a protégé of RAND nuclear-war-fighting theorist Albert Wohlstetter. Wolfowitz saw nuclear proliferation as the true global threat during his education at Chicago University. In his dissertation, Wolfowitz wrote that nuclear weapons in the Middle East would be a matter of "gravest concern." [7] He later joined Richard Perle in the office of Washington State Senator Henry "Scoop" Jackson and entered a darker, less theoretical world where he moved massive amounts of taxpayer dollars through hype, illusion, and fear-driven defense contracts.

In 1974, Wolfowitz contrived to convince Congress that there was a military "spending gap" between the US and the Soviet Union, requiring the US to "catch up." His approach comparing US military spending as a percentage of GDP in steady state with Soviet spending rocketing off the top of the chart is eerily similar to a comparison by the Project for the New American Century (PNAC, a neocon think tank) two decades later in the report "Rebuilding America's Defenses." But this similarity to later neoconservative tactics did not end with comparative GDP charts. The neoconservative strategy of manipulating and finessing intelligence to suit predetermined goals was first championed by Paul Wolfowitz.

Wolfowitz mentor Albert Wohlstetter and US Air Force Generals George Keegan and Daniel Graham attempted to gain access to raw CIA intelligence data covering Soviet military might and production. In a refrain that in many ways resembles pre-invasion claims about Iraq WMD, Wohlstetter and Wolfowitz claimed that the "CIA systematically underestimated the Soviet nuclear weapons stockpile in its annual National Intelligence Estimates." [8] They were quickly supported and promoted by a plethora of military contract-minded legislators in Congress demanding an alternative and objective independent "threat assessment" authored by unbiased "outside experts" unafraid of revealing true threats to America.

The CIA rejected the neocons' request for raw intelligence, but was overruled in 1976 when George H.W. Bush entered as CIA director and finally delivered raw intelligence to the outside group. The subsequent reports that Wolfowitz and his teammates delivered were as fantastical as they were flawed.

They forecast that the Soviet Union would deploy about 500 nuclear-armed Backfire bombers by 1984. In reality, Backfires did not number over 200 until 1996.[9] They also claimed that the Soviet Union was working on a new stealth submarine. Just as neoconservatives argued that Iraqi WMDs must have been shipped to Syria because none could be found in Iraq, lack of evidence about the "stealth submarine" transmogrified into definitive proof of its existence and the need for countermeasures. The neocons claimed that the absence of evidence meant the submarine was probably already deployed.[10] The authors of the outside report imagined immense Soviet nuclear stockpiles far outnumbering the US arsenal and created what is now known to be a completely false picture of a Soviet Union armed to the teeth and capable of dominating the world. In hindsight, most of their analysis was fanciful, contrived, and wholly inaccurate.

There is another important parallel between the case of the missing Soviet juggernaut and the neocon case for invading Iraq. When the neocons' Soviet juggernaut reports were entirely rejected and ignored by the incoming Carter administration, they didn't give up. Rather, they took their battle to the press and mass media, ultimately calling for congressional hearings, even as the Soviet Union's economy continued to weaken and then teeter on the brink of collapse.

Decades later, members of the Project for the New American Century would also take their case for invading Iraq to the public by releasing an open letter to President Clinton on January 26, 1998. (See Appendix A.) The PNAC letter demanded that Clinton commit to regime change in Iraq in his upcoming State of the Union address, since absence of evidence meant Saddam Hussein was up to something: "Our ability to ensure that Saddam Hussein is not producing weapons of mass destruction, therefore, has substantially diminished." The PNAC letter also frankly and openly referenced three core neoconservative concerns: troop logistics, Israel, and oil supplies.

"It hardly needs to be added that if Saddam does acquire the capability to deliver weapons of mass destruction, as he is almost certain to do if we continue along the present course, the safety of American troops in the region, of our friends and allies like Israel and the moderate Arab states, and a significant portion of the world's supply of oil will all be put at hazard." **PNAC letter to President Clinton, 11/26/1998**[11]

Paul Wolfowitz had attempted to incorporate a radical new doctrine of preemption into the US National Security Strategy as a Reagan-era DOD appointee, but failed. Reviewers and policymakers alike believed that a core strategy based on first strikes against hazy threats was too blunt an instrument, would not always "fit the crimes" of the targeted nation, and relied too heavily on sketchy and unreliable intelligence to be practical.[12] However, many neoconservatives still believe that even if a first strike is unleashed against the wrong country, it can still have benefits, no matter what the expense or damage to America's reputation.

"Every ten years or so, the United States needs to pick up some small crappy little country and throw it against the wall, just to show the world we mean business." **Michael Ledeen, American Enterprise Institute** [13]

# First-Strike Mythology and the 1967 Six-Day War

Neoconservatives' enduring infatuation with and mythology of military preemption is based on their understanding of the "success" of the 1967 Israeli first strike against the Egyptian Air Force. The 1967 Israeli-Arab war is heralded in bestselling books such as Michael Oren's *Six Days of War* and continually cited in the print media and even on American radio talk shows as definitively proving that military preemption works.

"Thirty-five years ago, on June 5, 1967, war broke out between Israel and three of its Arab neighbors. In a mere six days, the Israelis captured the Sinai Peninsula and the Gaza Strip from Egypt, the Golan Heights from Syria, and the West Bank of the Jordan River from the Kingdom of Jordan. The Six Day War's outcome set the stage for all subsequent relations between Arabs and Israelis. In time for this anniversary a book has appeared that- drawing on interviews and archival research in Israel, Egypt, the United States and Russia - gives as complete an account of the 1967 war as is ever likely to be written. In addition to providing the definitive history of that conflict, Michael B. Oren's "Six Days of War" offers a valuable perspective on the current troubles in the region." **Council on Foreign Relations**[14]

The mythology of a small, susceptible Israel surrounded and attacked by superior and hostile foes is repeated endlessly in the US news media by pundits and supporters:

"...prior to 1967 Palestine was controlled by Great Britain, and the land was divided into Jordan and Israel, Jordan was designated as the land for the Palestinians, and all the land to the west of the Jordan River was Israel for the Jews. Let's not forget the only reason that Israel controls the Gaza Strip and the West Bank is because she was attacked by Egypt, Jordan and Syria, and confiscated the lands as spoils of the war." **Radio host Armstrong Williams**[15]

The concept that Israel is justified in keeping the territorial spoils of war as compensation for an unprovoked and unavoidable attack reaches up into the highest levels of the US Department of Defense.

"My feeling about the so-called occupied territories are that there was a war, Israel urged neighboring countries not to get involved in it once it started, they all jumped in, and they lost a lost of real estate to Israel because Israel prevailed in that conflict. In the intervening period, they've made some settlements in various parts of the so-called occupied area, which was the result of a war, which they won." **Donald Rumsfeld, August 6, 2002**[16]

What Michael Oren's book about the 1967 war fails to mention, as do most other observers and writers, is that the Israeli attack didn't prevent an attack from Israel's enemies— on the contrary, it guaranteed a war that otherwise would never have occurred. We now know this thanks to the release of previously classified Johnson administration documentation and diplomatic cables released from the US State Department Office of the Historian on January 12, 2004 (see Appendix B). Few historians have updated their work to incorporate the stark diplomatic realities documented in the days leading up to war.

While Israel did attack Egyptian forces, it did so in full possession of intelligence that Egypt was attempting to wind down the crisis through shuttle diplomacy with Israel's largest foreign supporter, the United States.

The buildup to the crisis began with Palestinian attacks on Israel from bases located in Syria. This led to increasing Israeli insecurity, and missteps and blunders in the "fog of war" quickly escalated into a crisis. Syria believed that Israel would invade, and looked to Egypt for support. Egypt responded by moving troops into the Sinai Peninsula and ordering the withdrawal of UN peacekeeping forces. Amid escalating threats from both Israeli and Arab sides, Jordan then signed a mutual defense treaty with Egypt.

Israel launched a preemptive strike against the three Arab states on June 5, 1967, capturing the Sinai Peninsula, Gaza Strip, West Bank of the Jordan River, Old City of Jerusalem, and the Golan Heights. Neoconservative and Israeli lore embedded in most historical accounts hails this as an unavoidable and heroic response to imminent attack while discounting what was actually happening on the Arab and US diplomatic front. Another typical history book about the war, *Six Days in the Sun,* makes this clear:

> "It is of only academic interest now whether the Egyptian aircraft that the Israelis claim to have seen on their radar screens just before the attack was launched were really bent on aggressive moves against Israel, or whether they were the routine early morning patrols of whose timing the Israelis were fully aware from earlier intelligence missions. The Israelis had no doubts about the war of destruction that the Arabs had planned for them. They acted first—and left the questioning to the gentlemen at United Nations headquarters who had more time for such things and whose countries were not subject to daily threats of annihilation." *Six Days in the Sun*[17]

Many testosterone-drenched chronicles of this conflict must now be rewritten. Those previously classified US State Department documents released by the Office of the Historian on January 12, 2004[18] entirely refute the "heroic Israeli preemption in the face of long odds and inevitable attack." narrative. The previously classified chronology of secret Johnson administration communications reveals laborious Egyptian efforts to wind down the military escalation and vain US attempts to restrain the Israeli "tiger" from a first strike.

> "June 2, 1967, Egyptian President Nasser promised the US administration that he would not strike first, but was anxious about being overrun by Israel necessitating an Egyptian military mobilization into the Egypt's Sinai. Nasser stated that he did not want repetition of 1956 when he was 'reluctant to believe that an attack had begun and was slow in moving troops to Sinai only to be caught between the Israelis in the north and the British at Port Said.' He said he had no other choice but to mobilize and send troops

to Sinai in a defensive posture, but critically, that he would not begin any fight but would wait until the Israelis had moved." **Newly declassified Johnson administration papers**[19]

Israel was then instructed by the US to wait and not to act rashly by attacking Egypt.

On June 3, 1967, while arranging a diplomatic visit with President Johnson, Nasser again guaranteed that Egyptian troops in the Sinai were defensive positions designed to deter an Israeli invasion. Johnson apparently believed him. On June 3, 1967, President Johnson issued a strong warning about territorial integrity to Israeli Prime Minister Eshkol.

> "Our position in this crisis rests on two principles which are vital national interests of the United States. The first is that we support the territorial integrity and political independence of all of the countries of the Middle East. This principle has now been affirmed by four American Presidents. I must emphasize the necessity for Israel not to make itself responsible for the initiation of hostilities. Israel will not be alone unless it decides to go alone. We cannot imagine that it will make this decision." **Newly declassified Johnson administration papers**[20]

The US circulated a secret memorandum to US embassies in Arab states on June 3, 1967 expressing frustration over the level of control the US could actually expect to exert over Israel.

> "You should not assume that the United States can order Israel not to fight for what it considers to be its most vital interests. We have used the utmost restraint and, thus far, have been able to hold Israel back. But the 'Holy War' psychology of the Arab world is matched by an 'apocalyptic psychology' within Israel." **Newly declassified Johnson administration papers**[21]

## Deadly Dogma:
### How Neoconservatives Broke the Law to Deceive America

On June 4, 1967, Secretary Dean Rusk, Secretary of Defense Robert McNamara, National Security Council Special Representative Walt Rostow, and Ambassador Thompson began preparations for the visit of Egyptian Vice President Mohieddin and discussed ways to "hold the Israeli 'tiger'". The secretary of state informed the Israeli ambassador of Mohieddin's visit.

The Israeli cabinet discussed Mohieddin's visit and the likely fallout if Mohieddin's peace mission became public knowledge.[22]   The June 6, 1967 Israeli first strike effectively thwarted the exhaustive US diplomatic efforts and the inevitable gradual demobilization of Arab military forces. Israel's first strike created immense territorial issues and hard feelings that endure to the present day, including Israel's occupation of Old Jerusalem and large portions of the West Bank.  Israel's ongoing brutal occupation of these Palestinian lands is also a documented generator of suicide terrorism in retaliation against Israel and the US.[23]

The damage done to US interests is that by later enshrining and embedding that mythologized "first strike" into the US national security strategy, neocons have forced Americans to embrace the idea that first strikes work.  1967 is proof that first strikes rapidly and irreversibly sweep diplomatic options off the table. Although first strikes are easily supported by deceptions of the day that can take decades to debunk, first strikes limit diplomacy in crisis by reducing the amount of time available for effective negotiations.

Worse, first-strike strategies increase the likelihood that disingenuous intelligence, manipulation, and faulty analysis will be injected into the decision process by partisans of war. Wolfowitzian "stealth submarines" and other disinformation can suddenly loom large in the decision process. Unverifiable threats in the heady environment preceding a first strike suddenly become real.  The 1967 Israeli first strike, when viewed from the perspective of the newly released material, helps us better understand the hasty manipulations stoking the US invasion of Iraq.  Reality in both cases shows a confident aggressor, sure of achieving advantage for striking first, conducting empty diplomacy while assuring its population that war would be a last resort.

Israel was able to conflate a flare-up in its conflict with the PLO to seize strategic and "holy" territory it had long coveted, and do so in a manner that not only guaranteed military success but created a strong bid for internationally legitimate annexation. To date, only the Bush administration, spurred by Israel's politically active lobbies in the US, has hinted at legitimizing the Israeli annexations.

> "In light of new realities on the ground, including already existing major Israeli population centers, it is unrealistic to expect that the outcome of final status negotiations will be a full and complete return to the armistice lines of 1949." **George W. Bush, 1/14/2004** [24]

Before the first strike, Israeli intelligence analysts and government officials funneled a constant stream of disinformation to the Johnson administration that grossly inflated the military superiority of its Arab neighbors in order to secure more military funding and equipment from the United States. CIA analysts debunked Israel's analysis and relayed corrected information to the Johnson administration, which allowed it to dismiss and ignore false Israeli claims.[25]

In the long term, the disinformation campaign accompanying the war would color history. Israel seized the moment to launch the war in a way that allowed it to market its land captures within the "embattled valiant nation fighting for survival in the face of long odds" framework that endures to this day. The Johnson administration was not politically able to restrain Israel, implement US policy, or explain its true reservations about Israeli aggression to the American public. Israel then mined audiences persuaded by the embattled-nation mythology for additional charitable donations, political support for military aid that the false Israeli intelligence could not secure from Johnson, and propagation of an attractive strategic myth about the glories of military preemption that endures in books and policy circles.

# The Hidden Benefits of First-Strike Doctrine

In the US, neocon enshrinement of these 1967 mythologies does more than pull the American six-shooter out of its holster: the preemption doctrine installs a hair-trigger on the entire US military. This increases the probability that the US will fire on the wrong enemy without due consideration and deliberation.

Most Americans would consider the US invasion of Iraq, executed on the false pretext of disarming a hostile country stockpiled with weapons of mass destruction, to be a case against preemption. In the twisted logic of neoconservative luminaries, even the monumental folly of striking Iraq on false pretexts is evidence of the need to shave down the hair-trigger further. Richard Perle, a key architect of the war in Iraq, explained the perils of waiting to a journalist as follows:

> "If you want to try to wait until the very last minute, you'd better be very confident of your intelligence because if you're not, you won't know when the last minute is. And so, ironically, one of the lessons of the inadequate intelligence of Iraq is you'd better be careful how long you choose to wait. I can't tell you when we may face a similar choice with Iran. But it's either take action now or lose the option of taking action." **Richard Perle, 2/4/2006** [26]

Taking options off the table and "throwing a country against the wall" by mistake are certainly in line with neoconservative sloganeering and punditry. However, they are inimical to a nation founded on the principles of life, liberty, and the pursuit of happiness that holds itself out as an example to the world. Adopting such cynical and deception-prone policies would re-shackle the American people to the monarchial tyranny of following unelected despots who are endlessly plotting wars of aggression for their own and others' purposes and selling them to America as the "defense of the nation."

Justifying a military action as a "first strike" or "preemption" is more difficult if it is later revealed that the supposed opponent, such as Egypt, was suing for peace. Therefore, there is a movement underway to maintain the mythologies present in pre-2004 texts about the Six-Day War. Relatively few have been updated to encompass the Johnson administration data. Editing battles rage at popular online encyclopedias such as Wikipedia, with updated entries reflecting the newly declassified data being erased by censors enamored of a simpler, earlier history.

This is because history matters. If it becomes the popular belief that Egypt—or Iraq—had no offensive intentions or capabilities, maintaining a preemption policy is more difficult. In these cases, the term "first strike" and "preemption" should be retired for more accurate terminology. If an opponent had no intention or capability of striking, the word "first" simply does not apply. However, neoconservatives continue to ardently defend both events as preemptive wars. Why? Because preemption has benefits…for neoconservatives.

Preemption has moved the lever of power away from a larger group of people monitoring quantitative and objective metrics, such as enemy troop movements, weapons deployment, or verifiable conspiracies, into the hands of a few dealing in the realm of the subjective. Even in the Reagan era, nuclear disarmament was governed by the doctrine of "trust, but verify."

Under the neoconservative dogma of preemption, the first strike is a decision to be made by well-placed neoconservatives, on a "trust me to verify" basis. America can now go to war based on only the advice of neoconservatives. The US will attack Iran if neoconservatives determine that the "time has come" and it has become a "threat to America." No quantitative measure of estimated WMD development capability, launchers, or intentions will be needed. The strike could come tomorrow simply because, as Richard Perle would say, "it's either take action now or lose the option of taking action."

Gradually, analysts and historians may begin to describe the US action in Iraq simply as the "invasion and occupation." However, an entire corpus of reliable documents and frank perspectives contained in secret cables and communications may never be released.

Over 55,000 public documents that were originally declassified and released in 1999 are now quietly being reclassified and, wherever possible, pulled from public view. Some relate to the Korean War and the early Cold War and could be as revealing in terms of the evolution of strategy and doctrine as the Johnson administration documents on the Six-Day War. Recently reclassified documents also include decades-old State Department reports.[27] If this "national security state" mentality and acceleration toward broader classification continues, today's secrets about the deliberations preceding the Iraq invasion may continue to be secret indefinitely.

Given the irreversible release of classified documents from the US State Department on the Israeli attacks of 1967, however, at some point in the future, historians may refer to 1967 as an "Israeli war of aggression" while explaining the escalation and tense situation on the ground. The costs of the occupation that follows military preemption with exposed ground forces, however, may ultimately attract more public attention that the original pretexts for war.

## *Occupying Ill-Gotten Territory*

Invasions and occupations based on first-strike theory can be burdensome to the national treasury and international stature of the occupier. In a move reminiscent of Israel's bid to annex territory captured in 1967, the Bush administration is quickly solidifying its hold on strategic ground in Iraq. The United States is constructing six permanent military bases in Iraq, which will have to be financed indefinitely. The US is suffering daily attacks on highways, pipelines, and refineries as insurgents attempt to dislodge the "foreign occupier." Israel's attempt to swallow the West Bank has been somewhat restrained by the lack of enough settlers to occupy the entire area and the difficulty of securing it against conventional and unconventional counterattack.

On the international front, Israel has been the object of UN resolutions, International Court of Justice rulings, and world condemnation for its occupation of Palestinian lands. Israel may ultimately have to come to grips with the reality that most nations will never accept Israeli annexation of the West Bank and East Jerusalem. Press statements by the acting head of Israel's ruling Likud party have indicated a desire to hold on to strategic territory:

> "Even though we're talking about a security fence, my instructions are that Gush Etzion and Maale Adumim remain an inseparable part of the State of Israel," **Ehud Ohlmert, acting Prime Minister, 2/7/2006** [28]

Like Israel, the United States is stuck with the financial burden of either defending occupied territory or retreating from it. Territories conquered on deceptive preemptive pretexts compound the costs of lost credibility with the hard costs of occupation.

# Dogma #2: Unlimited Military Spending

"Israel can under these conditions better cooperate with the U.S. to counter real threats to the region and the West's security. Mr. Netanyahu can highlight his desire to cooperate more closely with the United States on anti-missile defense in order to remove the threat of blackmail which even a weak and distant army can pose to either state. Not only would such cooperation on missile defense counter a tangible physical threat to Israel's survival, but it would broaden Israel's base of support among many in the United States Congress who may know little about Israel, but care very much about missile defense. Such broad support could be helpful in the effort to move the U.S. embassy in Israel to Jerusalem."
**Richard Perle, Douglas Feith, David Wurmser, et al., 1996**[29]

Brokering military contracts provides hundreds of millions of dollars to neoconservative think tanks and the personal bank accounts of leading neoconservatives. The potential of military contracts for negotiating power alone is on public display in the report of the "study group" that authored the "Clean Break" plan for Benjamin Netanyahu upon his election as prime minister of Israel in 1996. Americans Richard Perle, Douglas Feith, and David Wurmser drafted and explained the concept of pressuring the American Congress to move the US embassy to Jerusalem via missile defense contract intermediation. The neocons' ability to direct and profit from large amounts of US defense spending continues to provide them with unprecedented financial resources and raw political power that makes them almost impossible to challenge.

In 1996, after the "Clean Break" plan was circulated, Congress authorized $3.6 billion ($750 million more than was requested) for missile defense systems. At the same time, Perle, Feith, and Wurmser's power began to soar. (See Appendix C.)

# A New Century of Unwarranted Spending

Neoconservative influence on US defense strategy and procurement became stronger in the immediate post-Cold-War period, but truly began to accelerate in the years and months before the 2000 presidential election. In September 2000, a group of prominent neoconservatives from the Project for the New American Century (PNAC) delivered a spending contract-brokering gambit in the form of a policy position paper on future American military strategy. PNAC, located within the American Enterprise Institute building, employed neocons such as Robert Kagan, Devon Gaffney Cross, Bruce P. Jackson, and John R. Bolton, with William Kristol filling the position of chairman. Gary Schmitt was executive director of the Project.

Echoing the shrill tone of Wolfowitz's "outside" assessment of the 1980s "spending gap" between the US and the Soviet Union, PNAC's paper "Rebuilding America's Defenses" professed shock over the relatively low levels of military expenditures in the Clinton era:

## *Dogma #2: Unlimited Military Spending*

"Today, America spends less than 3 percent of its gross domestic product on national defense, less than at any time since before World War II—in other words, since before the United States established itself as the world's leading power—and a cut from 4.7 percent of GDP in 1992, the first real post-Cold-War defense budget. Most of this reduction has come under the Clinton Administration; despite initial promises to approximate the level of defense spending called for in the final Bush Administration program, President Clinton cut more than $160 billion from the Bush program from 1992 to 1996 alone. Over the first seven years of the Clinton Administration, approximately $426 billion in defense investments have been deferred, creating a weapons procurement "bow wave" of immense proportions." **PNAC, Rebuilding America's Defenses, 9/2000**[30]

The paper is clear about what the signatory neoconservatives considered to be adequate levels of military spending. A higher spending level had little to do with true threats to the United States, which were, in hindsight, entirely missed by the document. Rather, a high percentage of GDP was to be disbursed to all sorts of sophisticated weapons programs in an attempt to maintain "military superiority":

"The program we advocate—one that would provide America with forces to meet the strategic demands of the world's sole superpower—requires budget levels to be increased to 3.5 to 3.8 percent of the GDP." **PNAC, Rebuilding America's Defenses, 9/2000**[31]

Although it purported to critically review American military strategy, the PNAC paper could be called the "Military Contractor Full Employment Act." It found no savings and laughed off any concept that America could devote post-Cold-War "peace dividends" to non-military pursuits. Rater, PNAC viewed military spending as a low-stakes poker game that needed more blue chips to make the game interesting and profitable enough for neocons to play. Rather than cut obsolete programs or understand that new rivals could implement effective low-technology countermeasures to new US systems, such as improvised explosive devices (IEDs), the paper pushed big-ticket hardware and integrated system spending proposals. The perennial neocon obsession with adequate stockpiles of ballistic missiles, formerly needed as a deterrent against the Soviet Union, would now be expanded and marketed as a necessary counter to "rogue states":

> "Proliferation of ballistic missiles and weapons of mass destruction…may soon allow lesser states to deter U.S. military action by threatening U.S. allies and the American homeland itself." **PNAC, Rebuilding America's Defenses, 9/2000** [32]

Why we needed to add weapons to a stockpile already numbering in the thousands in order to deter small states with insignificant arsenals is not fully explained in "Rebuilding America's Defenses."

The document also perverts the English language by asserting the need for the US to "control" the "commons" of space. Most of us would define the "commons" as undivided land subject to the use of multitudes. However, PNAC sees the space "commons" as a new strategic high ground for the US to fence, plow, and seed with weapons, ignoring the fact that if we did so, other states would also rush in to fully weaponize space and shave more time off the hair-trigger.

> "CONTROL THE NEW 'INTERNATIONAL COMMONS' OF SPACE AND 'CYBERSPACE,' and pave the way for the creation of a new military service—U.S. Space Forces—with the mission of

space control." **PNAC, Rebuilding America's Defenses, 9/2000**[33]

Although no rival was posing a deep-water naval threat to the US, PNAC's policy prescriptions included expanding the US naval force; they also failed to cancel spending on Cold War relics such as the F-22 jet fighter, built to go head-to-head with Russian jet fighters.

> "MODERNIZE CURRENT U.S. FORCES SELECTIVELY, proceeding with the F-22 program while increasing purchases of lift, electronic support and other aircraft; expanding submarine and surface combatant fleets." **PNAC, Rebuilding America's Defenses, 9/2000**[34]

Reading "Rebuilding America's Defenses" five years later reveals more about the authors' financial and political ambitions in the year 2000 than it does about US military deficiencies. Although the study authors identified no specific threats in "East Asia" (much less controversial than saying "the Middle East," but close enough), they advocated increased American regional military presence and capability. In short, PNAC's seminal paper can now be seen as advocating a stealth pre-positioning of resources near the Middle East, like American POMCUS units in Europe in the Cold War, for unstated—but not unplanned—US military incursions into the region.

The "bow wave" analogy used in "Rebuilding America's Defenses" is apt, but not for the reasons stated by neoconservatives. In physics, the center of a real bow wave is a highly destructive region,[35] which in this case could actually sink the ship of state. America's true bow wave is not a set of dreamy integrated weapons systems endlessly promoted by neocon think tanks; rather, it is the excessive debt and misallocation of American tax dollars, industrial production, producer markets, and human and physical resources spent on the procurement of useless weapons systems for disastrous wars of choice. By promoting provocative weapons programs, such as space weapons, rather than signing non-proliferation or arms control treaties, neocons guarantee escalating arms races to justify limitless future spending and a lucrative intermediation role for themselves. In the end, the neocons won their year 2000 broker's fees for evangelizing unsustainable military spending, which has now rocketed far past their upper GDP target.

The massive $453 billion military spending bill passed by Congress in 2005 was equivalent to $1,528.34 per capita, or about 4% of forecast US GDP for 2005. Four cents of every dollar of production in the US was destined for military purposes with few potential civilian spin-offs.

As stipulated by PNAC, the defense bill pays for stealth fighters, submarines, and other high-tech Cold-War-era playthings that are touted by the military-industrial complex but have little present-day relevance to defending America from looming threats ranging from bird flu to global warming and more powerful hurricanes. The F/A-22 stealth fighter plane is fully funded at $3.2 billion for 25 aircraft. The joint strike fighter received $5 billion in research and development funds, and the F/A-18E/F fighter received $2.75 billion for 42 planes. The Virginia-class submarine received $1.6 billion and the DDX destroyer $1.8 billion, while the Littoral Combat Ship budget tripled from the requested $249 million for one ship to $689 million for three (a $19.3 million-per-unit volume discount for economies of scale).

In most neocon white papers, the Middle East remains the location of future conflicts, a truth that has logically seeped into the marketing and military contractor public relations psyche. The following ad depicts US Marines rappelling into a mosque in an undisclosed country from a tilt rotor V-22 Osprey.

## Boeing's Osprey Mosque Attack Advertisement
*(Source: National Journal Magazine, 9/24/2005)*

PNAC operates as a high-profile military spending brokerage network, but it was not the first to enter the field. Frank Gaffney is the personification of neocon profligacy on weapons systems and the neocon network's corruption of US military contracting, with a long record of radical military spending advocacy.

# Frank Gaffney and the Domino's Pizza of Policy

After leaving the post of deputy assistant defense secretary for the Reagan administration, Frank Gaffney founded the Center for Security Policy (CSP) in 1988. Gaffney's policy pitches were specifically tailored to promote the wares of giant defense contractors that in turn covered 20-25% of CSP's annual budget. Military contractors AlliedSignal Inc., Lockheed Martin, Northrop Grumman Corp., Rockwell, and Thiokol Corp. gave tens of thousands in tax-deductible contributions. [36] Gaffney was provided with the rest of his budget by right-wing Jewish groups and foundations such as the Irving I. Moskowitz Foundation. Moskowitz, an active financer of illegal West Bank settlements in the Palestinian territories, contributed $75,000 to CSP in 1995. This profitable fusion of militarism and Zionism would inspire many other neocon think tanks to enter the field.

Like all the stars of the neocon think tank constellation, the CSP unequivocally touted massive, even ridiculous, military budgets, blanket opposition to arms control and peace treaties, and opposition and undermining of United Nations peacekeeping missions while unabashedly championing expansionist Israeli causes. Gaffney's exaggeration of threats was synchronized to a constant drumbeat for more military spending even after the Cold War had ended. He alarmed former military officers and more mainstream think tanks:

## *Dogma #2: Unlimited Military Spending*

"I think his (Gaffney's) general world outlook is colored by his desire to continue to spend huge amounts of money on weapons that we no longer have a need for." **Vice Adm. John Shanahan (ret.)** 37

Lawrence Korb, a senior fellow at the Brookings Institution and a former assistant defense secretary in the Reagan administration, agreed that the hype and exaggeration in Gaffney's policy recommendations were out of line with real-world financial propriety.

"If Clinton said we're going to double the defense budget, Frank would say, 'Let's triple it.'" **Lawrence Korb**

The post-Cold-War climate was justifiably hostile to Gaffney's lavish spending proposals, but after the GOP congressional win in 1994, Gaffney made common cause with a number of GOP members of Congress, including Bob Livingston of Louisiana, the House Appropriations Committee chairman. Livingston became one of the most powerful advocates of missile defense system spending, a key neoconservative contract brokerage arena that would pay unlimited commissions while providing unlimited power.

Like Wolfowitz and Perle, Gaffney's training in the profitability of pitching unlimited military spending began on the staff of the "Senator from Boeing," Henry M. Jackson. He moved on to the Senate Armed Services Committee when its chairman was John Tower, R-Texas. In 1983, Gaffney reunited with Jackson protègé Richard N. Perle, then an assistant secretary for international security policy. Gaffney leveraged his "neocon network" to enter as the deputy assistant secretary for nuclear forces and arms control policy. Gaffney's luck ran out when a new secretary of defense reshuffled the deck and his allies Perle and Casper Weinburger both left the Pentagon. Gaffney himself left in November of 1987.

CSP didn't need to do as much thinking as other policy outfits; its collective mind was already made up. CSP was mainly designed to mass-produce and flood policy and media channels with pre-molded assertions and sloganeering while crowding out more serious or opposing debate. Even Richard Perle couldn't resist comparing the CSP operation to a fast-food joint where speed trumps nutritional value or quality:

> "What we need is the Domino's Pizza of the policy business. If you don't get your policy analysis in 30 minutes, you get your money back." **Richard Perle**[38]

When it started, CSP resembled a small Domino's Pizza franchise in more ways than one. With only a four-person staff, the operation fed a network of frenetic like-minded conservative thinkers and Reagan-era national security officials. The news media, always on the prowl for a free lunch, gorged on CSP's filling but unhealthy fare. CSP's revenues quickly climbed toward a million dollars a year.

9/11's jetliner-based attack on America was an example of the new low-tech threats that were completely missed by PNAC and Gaffney's CSP as they strove to ratchet American spending and weapons stockpiles back to Cold War levels. Even if an analyst or two did consider the threat of low-tech asymmetrical warfare, there was no private money, congressional power, or "inside the beltway" influence to be had studying countermeasures for that type of threat. "Star Wars" missile defense was the bread and butter of CSP; it trumped all. After one Gaffney diatribe on higher missile defense spending at the Cato Institute, a critic of Gaffney's outdated worldview couldn't restrain himself:

> "I don't know how one can justify a comparable buildup in the absence of a serious global threat to U.S. security. Gaffney tends to confuse low-level threats with the kind of lethal threat once posed by the Soviet Union." **Ted Galen Carpenter, Cato Institute**

Proposing troop level increases, body armor, or more innovative tactical training to counter low-level threats does not provide dollars or influence to neocons like Gaffney. Easy access to the cockpits of passenger liners was a vulnerability noticed by airline passengers and consumer activists, but never seriously explored in any neocon think tank study before 9/11. Improvised explosive devices and other low-tech warfare tactics flew beneath their radar, in spite of their lethality. Frank Gaffney himself unwittingly revealed that defense contractor dollars for a very limited number of existing programs had made him tone-deaf. The only notes he could hear were scales moving toward misallocated big-ticket military spending. He revealed this shortly after 9/11 in an article:

> "One widespread and pernicious illusion died a fiery death on September 11: The notion that America— the "world's only superpower"—was invulnerable and its people secure within their own borders against foreign attack was vaporized along with the World Trade Center towers, portions of the Pentagon and the hijacked jet aimed at the Capitol. It appears that two other dangerous illusions linger on, however. One involves the belief clung to by die-hard opponents of President Bush's efforts to develop and

deploy effective missile defenses that we can safely perpetuate our complete vulnerability to another, far more deadly attack from ballistic missiles. The second is, if anything, even more preposterous: The belief that there are some "good" terrorists with whom we can prudently make common cause, at least temporarily, in waging war against the "bad" terrorists responsible for the events of 9/11....It behooves President Bush and the Congress to work together to ensure that effective missile defenses are built and deployed at the earliest possible time and that any new alliance is made with fellow democracies who are victims of terrorism, not with terrorists who have violently assaulted them and us."
**Frank Gaffney**[39]

In Gaffney's twisted world, hijacked, fully-fueled jetliners used to strike buildings in the US were a prime argument for the CSP's largest cookie-cutter answer to global security threats: ballistic missile defense. Threats hatched in caves in Afghanistan for reasons he would not trouble himself to understand, which would have struck the US with or without missile defense, were of little interest except as a new attention-getter in a tired missile defense sales pitch. This is how Gaffney earns his commissions.

In common white-collar crime, kickbacks are paid to contracting officials in the victim entity after an uncompetitive bid has been steered to the outside contractor. In neocon military contract brokering, there is a strict policy of avoiding the appearance of quid pro quo. Disbursements take place years before a defense contract is won. If questioned, the supposedly nonprofit charitable institution soliciting donations will plead adherence to its founding principles (of unlimited military spending) and say that it is not just another unregistered lobbyist, although many neocons are lobbyists on the other side of the revolving door. Before he entered the Pentagon as undersecretary of defense for policy, Douglas Feith was a partner in the Washington law firm of Feith & Zell, which represented several defense contractors including Lockheed Martin.

# Military Contracts: A New Protection Racket

Protection rackets are complex crimes where the victim is not always a small business. A protection racket is an extortion scheme whereby a powerful organization, especially a criminal organization or gang, coerces individuals or businesses to pay money that allegedly purchases the organization's "protection" services against various external threats—but the actual threat comes from the organization itself. Those who do not buy into the protection plan are often targeted by the organization and harassed to force payment of the protection money.

> The protection money is typically collected by a "Bag Man." Although the organization might be particularly coercive in obtaining protection money, it usually attacks other organizations that tries to solicit or similarly threaten the targeted individuals or businesses, which often arises out of disputes between organizations concerning "turf" or territory."[40]

The neighborhood grocery store that agrees to pay the bagman in an extortion racket is not the ultimate victim. The customers who pay higher prices for products after the store raises prices to cover the extra overhead are the ultimate victims.

## Deadly Dogma:
### How Neoconservatives Broke the Law to Deceive America

Few would say that a protection racket isn't really a crime because its ill-gotten gains are spread so widely. A criminal prosecutor, likewise, would not be swayed by the bagman's argument that many businesses are willing participants in protection rackets—after all, the service ostensibly extended by the local mobster is "protection."

In reality, a protection racket is a blight on the neighborhood. It undermines the authority and role of the police while giving greater power to criminals' other rackets. Even if the bagman becomes a charitable benefactor in the community, his protection racket does not suddenly become legal.

Frank Gaffney and other neocons are bagmen in a sophisticated protection and coercion racket involving Congress, military contractors, and foreign influences. Their real victims are US taxpayers. When pushed against the wall, the bagman and his supporters will squeal that their views are "honestly held," even if constantly wrong, and that they have a "right to be heard."

The result of the neocons' inflationary threat assessments is that Paul Wolfowitz and Frank Gaffney have committed massive fraud against US taxpayers. Their truly flawed "hockey-stick-shaped" growth curves for wasteful military spending and fanciful threats such as "stealth submarines," made in the absence of any evidence, constitute outright fraud, whether or not the authors convince themselves of their veracity. They have touched off arms races where none needed to exist. But just as the crime boss believes he's just "cleaning up the neighborhood," neocon hubris allows no room for admitting crimes or mistakes. Even so, the evidence of fraud remains on the record. The pattern of misleading, uncorrected, and wildly overblown threat analysis strongly resembles corporate accounting fraud, except that "shareholders in America," US taxpayers, were defrauded, and money wasn't the only thing of value lost. The neocon defense contract extortion racket has cost more than 100,000 Iraqi lives, trillions of dollars, and America's good reputation.

# The Boeing Tanker Leasing Deal

One of the most brazen attempts to extort through a military-industrial-neocon protection racket was the Boeing tanker leasing scandal of 2003. In 2001, Boeing Corporation proposed to lease, rather than sell, a hundred aerial refueling tankers based on the 767 airframe. The deal was suspicious for three reasons: No credible outside evaluation of the need for tankers was performed, nor were options such as fleet upgrade considered. The fact that the 767 tankers wouldn't be able to refuel multiple aircraft simultaneously or serve for other missions, such as medical evacuations, was irrelevant to the neocon marketing plan.[41] The deal was initially structured as a lease, and later a hybrid that would allow leasing and purchase of the tankers at a far higher price than outright purchase. Apparently unaware of the government's ability to issue medium- and long-term bonds at interest rates far more attractive than commercial leasing rates, Paul Wolfowitz, Richard Perle, and a cadre of neoconservatives publicized the deal as extremely beneficial to the cash flow of the United States.

> The leasing deal "strikes the necessary balance between the critical need for new air-refueling tankers and the constraints on our budget." **Paul Wolfowitz, 11/7/2003** [42]

Boeing spread money far and wide to push the $27 billion leasing deal through Congress and the Pentagon. Some of it went into a broad public relations campaign, including "education" sessions for neocon think tanks such as the American Enterprise Institute and Center for Security Policy.

> "Rarely has an acquisition been more necessary, however, than is the case with aerial-refueling tankers. Such aircraft are the sine qua non of U.S. power projection. As the recent efforts to liberate Afghanistan and Iraq have underscored, the rapid and sustained deployment of American forces to the world trouble-spots depends heavily on airlift. Airlift, in turn, depends critically on tankers. Shortfalls in the tanker fleet very rapidly translate, literally, into an inability to support the troops."
> **Frank Gaffney, 9/3/2003** [43]

Boeing's political action committee targeted dollars to supportive candidates; other Boeing dollars were even more targeted. Richard Perle sought and received $20 million from Boeing while the deal was still in the concept stage to be invested in his venture capital firm, Trireme Partners LLP.[44] Perle was a managing partner of this Delaware company, which was incorporated in November of 2001.

Boeing's private investment in Perle paid off handsomely, as he ramped up his public and private lobbying for the leasing deal and fought against those questioning the cost and concept of government leasing on such a massive scale.

> "Some in Congress have also grumbled about the tanker-lease innovation. Even some lawmakers who have strongly supported rebuilding America's defenses take a narrow and disparaging view of the Air Force's proposal. Maybe they have—but have not yet revealed—a better way to meet the urgent

> need for extending the effective range of the Air
> Force that protects us." **Richard Perle, 8/4/2003**[45]

The outrageous price of the lease, far exceeding the cost of outright purchase, was noted internally in Boeing executive emails sent to dozens of top executives.

> "Briefly, the OMB (Office of Management and Budget) A-94 Business Case Analysis will most likely pass the test. But this test measures the illogical conclusion that it is better to lease now than to buy now. This won't make sense in the newspapers. Further, neither Boeing nor SSMB (Salomon Smith Barney) would ever put its hand on a Bible and say that makes economic sense." **Walter Skowronski, Boeing Vice President for Finance and Treasurer**[46]

Ultimately, an investigation by the Inspector General's office found that the Boeing lease contract was based on an invalid specifications document that didn't meet the real needs of the armed forces.[47] Arizona Republican Senator John McCain, who chaired the U.S. Senate Commerce, Science, and Transportation Committee as well as serving on the Senate Armed Services Committee, strongly opposed the deal. McCain investigated the deal and the corruption surrounding the negotiations, including chief Air Force tanker negotiator Darleen Druyun's subsequent employment at Boeing and other questionable financial transactions. Internally, Boeing believed it had bought and paid for a reliable Air Force operative through a lucrative job and relocation offer.

> "Meeting today on price was very good. Darleen (Druyun, then still an Air Force official) spent most of the time bringing the USAF (U.S. Air Force) pricer up to our number....It was a good day. She may be running her own covert operation on this one, so we probably don't want to discuss openly." **Boeing tanker chief Bob Gower**[48]

Druyan later went to prison for negotiating a job with Boeing while simultaneously overseeing multiple proposals from the military contractor.

A final Pentagon Inspector General (IG) report released to the Senate in June of 2005 revealed the extent of corruption at the heart of the deal. The report rejected earlier claims by the Air Force and outside pundits that new tankers were urgently needed because the older fleet allegedly suffered major corrosion problems.[49] The final IG report also found that the Air Force had reduced necessary war-fighting capabilities for the planned tanker lease in order to match capabilities demonstrated by an existing Italian military 767 tanker, rather than the actual requirements of the US armed forces.

The neocon network that worked to conceptualize and market the deal completely escaped criminal prosecution. Boeing CEO Philip Condit and other executives stepped down, and Boeing's former chief financial officer Mike Sears pled guilty to illegally hiring Darleen Druyan.

The neocon hucksters promoting the deal for profit quietly rowed away from the scene; thus, the name of the Perle venture, Trireme, is oddly appropriate. The trireme (Greek root is *trieres*) was an ancient battleship designed to cover long distances quickly under oar as well as sail. In battle, a trireme could ram and severely damage other ships. In Richard Perle's world, the American people and their tax dollars are clearly at the oars of his corrupt ventures. No matter that a military contract is rife with corruption and does not meet real military needs. The neocons urge us to row on, but at what cost?

# *The Cost of Neocon Intermediation*

The cost of neocon intermediation of US military contracts is high. Inappropriate hardware and systems are pitched, the news media is mobilized, Congress is pressured, and American industry is tasked with producing wasteful output. The ultimate victim is the US taxpayer, who has little say in the policies that determine American defense strategy.

Putting a figure on the total cost of neocon intermediation in defense contracts is difficult. While lobbyists and members of Congress must disclose lobbying activities and campaign fees, neoconservative military brokers, operating out of a raft of nonprofit think tanks and "consulting" and "advising" contracts, are completely opaque. There is simply no way to determine exactly what percentage of America's total military spending ultimately winds up in the hands of neocon brokers.

However, if we do want to arrive at a rough estimate, a useful starting point is Richard Perle's Boeing fee. Though it was structured as an "investment" in a "venture capital fund," there was no restriction on Perle's drawing Boeing's gift down to zero through expenses and "management fees." By structuring the disbursement as an "investment," Boeing can carry the commission as an asset on its balance sheet. By receiving the commission as a Trireme "investment," Perle can draw upon the $20 million, earn interest, and spend the proceeds as tax-free "business expenses" rather than taxable income.

If other neocon military brokers are demanding approximately the same fees as Perle, the commission rate is .0741%, which is not very exciting compared to the 5-7% commission charged by the average real estate broker.

However, small groups of real estate brokers rarely move properties worth US $513 billion per year. $513 billion is the official proposed US defense budget for 2006.[50] At the rate of .0741%, neocon military contract brokers would stand to pull $380 million in unreported speaking fees, think tank endowments, "consulting" work, "venture capital investments," and research grants. This is $100 million more than the South American nation of Uruguay spends on its yearly defense budget.

Some might say that $380 million is a reasonable price to pay for "good advice" and the ability to "see the future." But most would rather not talk about it. Even when asked directly, top military contractor Northrop Grumman CEO Ron Sugar would not reveal how much company revenue is dedicated to neocon military brokerage commissions.

> "Grant F. Smith: I've got a quick question. We've just emerged from a period where financial analysts on Wall Street created a particular set of problems for the small investor, for being too close to the industry. It seems to many outsiders...
>
> Ron Sugar, CEO Northrop Grumman: Are you referring to the research report that caused the market caps to all plunge?
>
> Grant F. Smith: No, I'm referring to just too much communication between the so-called "analysts"....
>
> Ron Sugar, CEO Northrop Grumman: Oh.
>
> Grant F. Smith:...and the industry. In the interest of disclosure, and allaying these fears to the American people now, when defense purchases are so critical, could you give us an idea, and this is as much for the AEI people as you, how much of the policy research, telling us who we should shoot at, and what we

should shoot at them with, particularly produced by Mr. Perle, how much of this AEI policy research is being funded by the defense industry?

Your (American Enterprise Institute) Schedule B forms on the (IRS) 990's don't really tell the public where the money is coming from. And just in the interest of full and fair disclosure, I think it's a critical thing to disclose. Thank you.

Ron Sugar, CEO Northrop Grumman: Yeah. I don't know the specific numbers. I can assure you that the, there is an enormous value to, for companies like mine and others to work with all sources of intellectual capital around the, company, country rather, and sometimes outside the country, both in terms of technological advice and policy advice. If you think about our thoughts about the future a decade ago, if we were simply hunkered down in lab coats with our noses to our test tubes, we wouldn't have figured out that there was major policy shifts that would change the future of warfare. Which means we should retool and reinvest our company in a certain direction. So having good input from outsiders is important, at the end of the day we have to make the decision as to what we do with it. And yes in fact, if we ask for studies to be done, we will pay for them to be done. I don't have any figures about how much money we are spending today." **American Enterprise Institute conference, "Transforming the Military Industrial Complex," 10/10/2003**[51]

In reality, Boeing and Northrop don't actually pay for neocon brokerage commissions. Every fatally flawed proposal for refueling tankers that won't work, nonexistent stealth submarine countermeasures, and grossly inflated annual defense budgets is paid for by deceived American taxpayers.

# Dogma #3: The Nobility of Lies

"We know that he has the infrastructure, nuclear scientists to make a nuclear weapon. And we know that when the inspectors assessed this after the Gulf War, he was far, far closer to a crude nuclear device than anybody thought—maybe six months from a crude nuclear device. The problem here is that there will always be some uncertainty about how quickly he can acquire nuclear weapons. But we don't want the smoking gun to be a mushroom cloud."
**Condoleeza Rice** [52]

"The truth is that for reasons that have a lot to do with the U.S. government bureaucracy we settled on the one issue that everyone could agree on which was weapons of mass destruction as the core reason..."
**Paul Wolfowitz** [53]

Neoconservatives are willing to stage massive disinformation and propaganda campaigns to advance their interests. This sets them apart from other political interest groups that prefer to make arguments based on more solid evidence. However, their use of "noble" strategic lying is based on the belief that sometimes people need to be fooled into supporting policies that they would not support on the merits of the policy. The strategy of the Noble Lie was popularized among neocons by an intellectual grandfather and has become an indispensable tool for them to wield against the American public.

## Deadly Dogma:
### How Neoconservatives Broke the Law to Deceive America

The biggest Noble Lie to be exposed so far is the disinformation campaign that provided a pretext for the US invasion of Iraq. Americans now know, from the release of information such as the confidential Downing Street Memos published by The Sunday Times in the UK on May 1, 2005, that high-level Bush administration officials were "fixing intelligence around policy." The Downing Street Memo is a transcript of a meeting with the British prime minister on July 23, 2002. The top-secret memo summarized the Bush administration's intention to invade Iraq as it was communicated to UK officials and PM Tony Blair:

> "There was a perceptible shift in attitude. Military action was now seen as inevitable. Bush wanted to remove Saddam, through military action, justified by the conjunction of terrorism and WMD. But the intelligence and facts were being fixed around the policy. The NSC had no patience with the UN route and no enthusiasm for publishing material on the Iraqi regime's record. There was little discussion in Washington of the aftermath after military action."
> **Downing Street Memo**[54]

This transcript was hard evidence backing what many in the UK and US already believed from more circumstantial evidence and the daily news: that their governments misrepresented the pretexts for invading Iraq. The antiseptic and brutally honest assessment in the Downing Street Memo revealed the Bush administration's unstoppable push for war and the neocons' blasé approach to post-bellum Iraq. The chaos and bloodshed consuming Iraq today were not unforeseen by major neoconservative pundits.

> "One can only hope that we turn the region into a cauldron, and faster, please. If ever there were a region that richly deserved being cauldronized, it is

the Middle East today. If we wage the war effectively, we will bring down the terror regimes in Iraq, Iran, and Syria, and either bring down the Saudi monarchy or force it to abandon its global assembly line to indoctrinate young terrorists. That's our mission in the war against terror." **Michael Ledeen, 2002** [55]

Invading Iraq and toppling Saddam Hussein was a core neoconservative policy goal, endlessly repeated in policy position papers, books, talks, and interviews with leading neoconservatives. The invasion was ultimately sold on false pretexts, since no sane American would support an invasion in the name of creating a "cauldron" in the Middle East or securing supposed Israeli objectives. Saddam Hussein of Iraq was certainly terrible, but he was effectively contained from the standpoint of US security concerns. Saddam Hussein had no offensive capability in the Middle East, no chemical, biological, or nuclear weapons, and most importantly, no connection whatsoever to the terrorist attacks of 9/11.

None of this mattered to Straussian neocons.

The Bush administration (or more specifically, Richard Cheney) brought in eight neocons with longstanding records of advocating Iraqi regime change after the 2000 presidential election. Richard Perle, David Wurmser, and Douglas Feith argued that Hussein needed to be toppled and replaced with a Hashemite monarch as an Israeli strategic objective in their 1996 consulting paper to Prime Minister Benjamin Netanyahu. This Israeli objective predated 9/11 by a half-decade, and was only clumsily integrated into George W. Bush's "war on terrorism" after the attack.

Most of Cheney's advisory group members belonged to the Project for the New American Century or the Israel-based Institute for Advanced Strategic and Political Studies.

PNAC's focus on repositioning US military assets into East Asia was a logical progression of the "Clean Break" attack plan.

## Iraq War Planners Surrounding Bush and Their PNAC /IASPS Backgrounds
*(Source: Zfacts)*[56]

| PNAC: Lobbied for Iraq War from 1998 on | | |
|---|---|---|
| **Kristol** | PNAC Chair, top neocon | |
| **Cheney** | Vice President | Top Nine Iraq War Architects Under Bush |
| **Rumsfeld** | Secretary of Defense | |
| **Wolfowitz** | Deputy Defense Secretary | |
| **Abrams** | White House staff | |
| **Libby** | Cheney's Chief of Staff | |
| **Bolton** | State Department | |
| **Perle** | Defense Policy Board Chair | |
| **Feith** | Under Secretary of Defense | |
| **Wurmser** | Cheney staff | |
| **Fairbanks** | Wolfowitz associate | zFacts.com |
| IASPS: Authors of 1996 report explaining why Israel needs Saddam removed from power | | |

# From Leo Strauss to the Great WMD Hoax of 2002

Selling the US invasion of Iraq to the American people before the attacks of 9/11 would probably have been impossible. However, in the years before 9/11, many neocons were on the lookout for a useful violent calamity or other negative catalyst to force US military spending back to Cold War levels and enable their planned intervention in Iraq.

> "...the process of transformation, even if it brings revolutionary change is likely to be a long one, absent some catastrophic and catalyzing event—like a new Pearl Harbor." **PNAC, Rebuilding America's Defenses**[57]

9/11 was effectively harnessed to transform American fear of terrorist attacks into popular support for invading Iraq. The driving mechanism was the willingness of neoconservative operatives in government, media, and policy circles to propagate Noble Lies designed to motivate the populace by connecting Iraq and 9/11. The Weapons of Mass Destruction (WMD) campaign will someday be thought of as one of the biggest hoaxes ever perpetrated on an unwitting populace. Some former high-level officials are already quite clear about this:

> "I participated in a hoax on the American people, the international community, and the United Nations Security Council." **Lawrence Wilkerson, former Chief of Staff to Secretary of State Colin Powell**[58]

## Deadly Dogma:
### How Neoconservatives Broke the Law to Deceive America

Merriam-Webster defines *hoax* as "to trick into believing or accepting as genuine something false and often preposterous."[59] When entire gangs of confidence men and hucksters perpetrate a hoax for their own gain over electronic communications media, US law calls this wire fraud.

The later Noble Lie campaign claiming that CIA intelligence on Iraq was flawed began to fall flat when CIA officers explained how their product was actually used by the Bush administration:

> "It has become clear that official intelligence was not relied on in making even the most significant national security decisions, that intelligence was misused publicly to justify decisions already made, that damaging ill will developed between [Bush] policymakers and intelligence officers, and that the intelligence community's own work was politicized."
> **Paul R. Pillar, CIA national intelligence officer for the Near East and South Asia from 2000 to 2005** [60]

What was the intellectual underpinning of the neoconservatives' drive to perpetrate a massive hoax on the American people as a pretext for war? Many say that Leo Strauss, an intellectual who taught at the University of Chicago, popularized the utility of the Noble Lie among his eager students, including Paul Wolfowitz. The following neoconservatives are also considered "Straussian" for their strong identification with Leo Strauss' philosophy and teachings: George Anastaplo, Seth Benardete, Walter Berns, Allan Bloom, Charles Butterworth, Joseph Cropsey, Werner Dannhauser, Martin Diamond, Paul Eidelberg, Francis Fukuyama, Hilail Gildin, Harry V. Jaffa, Leon Kass, Irving Kristol, William Kristol, Ralph Lerner, Harvey Mansfield, Jr.,

## *Dogma #3: The Nobility of Lies*

Roger Masters, Thomas Pangle, Stanley Rosen, and Herbert Storing. [61]

When Strauss urged students to consider the utility of the Noble Lie and its role in society, he leaned heavily on the original author of the concept: Plato.

In *The Republic*, Plato described a city whose inhabitants were organized into three categories: Rulers, Auxiliaries, and Farmers. The Rulers (also called Guardians) would be recruited from the top military echelon for their skills at herding and caring for the community. Guardians-in-training would be promoted from the Auxiliaries.

The Rulers would legitimize their power, authority, and policies by telling the people of the city the "Noble Lie" that they were assigned to their ranks by divine intervention. God, they said, put gold, silver, or iron into each person's soul. These metals, and not the rulers, predetermined a person's station in life.

On a theoretical level, Plato argued that these lies were necessary to maintain a stable social structure and efficient workforce. In Plato's mind, the Noble Lie was a religious lie that was fed to the masses to keep them under control and happy with their situation in life, and was, in short, for their own good.

Plato did not believe that the majority of people were intelligent enough to look after society's or even their own best interests. An elite intelligentsia would lead the rest of the flock and receive remuneration for their trouble, and the Noble Lie would keep it all going.

> "No one is willing to govern; because no one likes to take in hand the reformation of evils which are not his concern without remuneration. For, in the execution of his work, and in giving his orders to another, the true artist does not regard his own interest, but always that of his subjects; and therefore in order that rulers may be willing to rule, they must

> be paid in one of three modes of payment: money, or honour, or a penalty for refusing." **Plato** [62]

The broad distribution and drumbeat of the Iraq WMD Noble Lie is now well documented and still sears many memories. The Fox News network, which aired more neocon pundits and administration officials shilling for invasion on fabricated grounds than any other American news network, fundamentally and quantifiably misinformed its US viewers. A PIPA/Knowledge Networks poll published in October 2003 revealed the following:

> "Those receiving most of their news from Fox News are more likely than average to have misperceptions. Those who receive most of their news from NPR or PBS are less likely to have misperceptions. These variations cannot simply be explained as a result of demographic characteristics of each audience, because these variations can also be found when comparing the demographic subgroups in each audience." **PIPA/Knowledge Networks Poll, 10/2003** [63]

Few are surprised these days when politicians or policymakers are caught lying on a small scale. What is truly surprising about the Iraq lie is that, once it was debunked by undeniable evidence that Iraq was not a WMD threat to the US or anyone else, new Noble Lies were immediately deployed to backfill the open question "Why did the US invade?"

# Poll: Do you think the Bush administration deliberately misled the American public about whether Iraq has weapons of mass destruction, or not?

*Source: Gallup / CNN / USA Today*
*Methodology: Telephone interviews with 1,006 American adults, conducted from Jan. 20 to Jan. 22, 2006. Margin of error is 3%.*

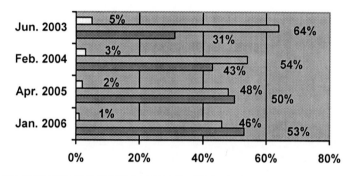

The realpolitik analysis in the original "Rebuilding America's Defenses" is that the US invaded for oil, Israel, and logistics. Controlling a vital petroleum-producing region would allow the US to "project power" and deny resources to others. Threats against Israel would be nullified by the US presence, and a strong message would be sent to Israel's regional opponents. US troops that had overstayed their welcome in Saudi Arabia could find new bases in Iraq. Finally, massive reconstruction of the damage wrought by Saddam Hussein and US bombing would provide an unlimited boon for US engineering firms and manufacturers, according to neocon thinking in 2003. All would be paid for with Iraqi oil revenue, making the invasion a kind of global "leveraged buyout" where equity in hard revenue assets would be purchased with

American bullets and a necessary investment of American lives.

> "There's a lot of money to pay for this that doesn't have to be U.S. taxpayer money, and it starts with the assets of the Iraqi people…and on a rough recollection, the oil revenues of that country could bring between $50 and $100 billion over the course of the next two or three years…We're dealing with a country that can really finance its own reconstruction, and relatively soon." **Undersecretary of Defense Paul Wolfowitz, 3/27/2003** [64]

In reality, Iraq was a bad investment. The fully loaded costs of the Iraq debacle are staggering if we include current and projected spending on combat and support operations, medical costs of treating injured veterans, disability wages, costs of demobilization, increased capital spending for defense and equipment replacement, replacement of consumables such as missiles, and interest payments on war debt in an era of slowly rising interest rates and less demand for US government obligations. Credible outside estimates place the cost of the Iraq war at $750 billion to $1.1 trillion, assuming a diminishing presence in Iraq for the next five years.[65]

Neoconservatives believed that the Iraq invasion case simply could not have been made to the American people based on rational, objective analysis and frank discussion. So it was made based on Noble Lies and neocon think tank propaganda that they continue to disseminate to this day, although relatively few Americans consider the results to be favorable. Americans' unprecedented levels of skepticism toward their own government and distrust of the corporate news media have created angst and malaise that may find destructive expressions in coming years, much like the post-combat stress syndrome breaking down thousands of veterans returning from the conflict zone.

Behind the scenes, neoconservative military contract brokers are busy writing up noncompetitive production-sharing agreements for Iraq with three-digit rates of return.[66] Richard Perle's cohort Gerald Hillman argued as a member of the Pentagon Defense Policy Board that Iraq's existing oil contracts with Russia, France, and other nations were invalid, and that the US would have to become the exclusive broker of Iraqi oil. Much of this neoconservative vision has become reality.

Petroleum companies also benefited from huge profit windfalls as Iraqi production remained off the world market. Neocon policymakers are now busily turning the ship of state toward Iran, while the Bush administration continues to crack down on Americans' constitutional rights in favor of a national-security-oriented state.

The neoconservatives and Noble Lie devotees who fought so hard for the invasion have felt no remorse that their pretexts for war are now popularly known as deliberate fabrications. New rationales, such as "democratizing the Middle East" or "overthrowing a brutal dictator," have been framed and launched to fill the WMD void. Critics of the costs of the ongoing occupation are told to grin and bear it: "Now that we're there, pulling out would be a disaster." This appalling logic adds injury to insult, the equivalent of the rapist counseling his victim not to think about the sordid crimes of the past, but rather look toward caring for the new baby. Neocons grudgingly realized the need to launch alternative rationales for the invasion, but not out of remorse; rather, they did so to protect neoconservative influence, pet projects, military contract commissions, and the host administration.

> "If the American people really come to a settled belief that Bush lied us into war, his presidency will be over. He won't have the basic level of trust needed to govern. His initiatives, domestic and foreign, will

founder. Support for the war on terror will wane."
**Bill Kristol** [67]

It may be too late for renewed credibility. The coordinated neoconservative attack on the truth struck hard at the heart of American ideals. The neocon willingness to cover lies with new lies publicly reveals neocons as corrupt and arbitrary power brokers who clearly hold most Americans in contempt.

## *The Consequences of Noble Lies*

In January of 2006, Bill Kristol's worst-case scenario of presidential credibility quantitatively came true. In a statistically significant poll, the majority of Americans (53%) believed that the Bush administration deliberately misled the American public about the pretext for invading Iraq.[68] Such a poisoned and weakened American civic environment is a rich growth medium for the bacillus of broader societal decay and reciprocal lawbreaking. When public figures are believed to be lying on a massive scale, it lowers the bar, and all lies seem less objectionable. While the idea that we can create a falsehood-free society is utopian, an immense unresolved lie about a major war promoted by top administration officials and revealed while they are still in office breaks entirely new ground. While other presidential administrations have been caught lying about pretexts for war, it has never happened during their watch, nor has word spread so quickly.

On November 30, 2005, the National Security Agency (NSA) released hundreds of pages of secret documents concerning US involvement in and insinuation into Vietnam's civil war. The Gulf of Tonkin incident of August 4, 1964 was actually a fabrication, according to NSA historian Robert J. Hanyok. Hanyok demonstrated that the NSA intelligence officers deliberately skewed intelligence evidence delivered to policymakers and the public in order to falsely suggest that North Vietnamese ships had attacked American destroyers in international waters.[69] Mr. Hanyok revealed that 90 percent of the most critical intercepts of North Vietnamese communications relevant to the time period of the incident, which would have revealed radar blips of torpedoes and enemy ships, were actually figments of skittish naval officers' imaginations, and were omitted from the corpus of critical NSA documents delivered to policymakers.[70]

Only now, thirty years too late, are the NSA and the Johnson administration undergoing more intense historical scrutiny by better-informed scholars, historians, and members of the public. From the current administration's point of view, it would have been much more convenient to have the WMD facts revealed thirty, or even ten, years in the future. Many administration officials still hold on to the fantasy of WMDs emerging from the sands of Iraq.

In reality, the administration failed ethicist Sissela Bok's simple cost-benefit analysis of the utility of telling fibs. Bok, the author of *Lying: Moral Choice in Public and Private Life*, proposed the following test: "Would I be able to explain this afterwards?" The benefit that the administration gained by lying was the immediate implementation of the Iraq invasion plan, a neocon objective that had been years in the making. The consequences of public knowledge of the invasion's faulty pretext, however, are now reflected in the polls: a president and administration with no public credibility. All major studies of lies in public policy reveal similar conclusions: no one likes to be deceived. Once a big lie is revealed, all future trust and credibility are lost. Studies document that such lies also promulgate lying by the victims, underlings, collaborators, and other stakeholders. If the top officials of America's elected government are lying to you, you won't feel so bad lying to the government on, say, your Form 1040, or to the city council, or on a government job application, or to the judge. The moral rot that begins at the top does not long remain there.

# Dogma #4: Plunder and Saturate Media Networks

"As a publisher I have to take full responsibility for everything that appears in my publications, whether I read them or not." **Mortimer Zuckerman of *US News and World Report*, former chair of the Conference of Presidents of Major Jewish Organizations (Response to a scholarly article in the Davos-sponsored *Global Agenda* magazine recommending divestment from Israel)** [71]

Media mogul Conrad M. Black's criminal indictment and ousting from Hollinger International caused a shockwave in neoconservative circles. Conrad Black served as the Chairman of the Board of Directors and Chief Operating Officer of Hollinger International Inc., while Richard Perle served on the Board of Directors.

At its height, Hollinger was a neoconservative media promotion empire owning and supporting a raft of influential newspapers and magazines. Hollinger still owns or has a stake in the *Chicago Sun-Times*, the *New York Sun*, and *La Republica*. Until the year 2004, Hollinger also owned the UK's *Daily Telegraph, Sunday Telegraph*, and *The Spectator*, as well as the *Jerusalem Post*. Hollinger International made an annual contribution of $200,000 to the *National Interest*, a conservative quarterly magazine tied to Richard Perle and Henry Kissinger. [72]

Heavy-handed editorial policymaking and promotion of neoconservative causes were Conrad Black's trademarks. Black set editorial policy at his newspapers and promoted editors with similar views. David Radler, Hollinger president and publisher of the *Chicago Sun-Times* and *Jerusalem Post*, clarified the roles of ownership and neocon ideology at Hollinger:

> "If editors disagree with us they should disagree with us when they're no longer in our employ. The buck stops with ownership. I am responsible for meeting the payroll; therefore I will ultimately determine what the papers say and how they're going to be run."
> **David Radler, 9/2003** [73]

Neocon ideology and militant Zionism commanded the editorial pages and editorial control at Hollinger publications. The *Jerusalem Post* openly advocated assassinating Palestinian leader Yasser Arafat in September of 2003, a policy that was given somber consideration by the Israeli Cabinet. Publisher David Radler clarified the paper's commitment to promoting Israeli causes:

> "Through different owners and different leaders, the *Chicago Sun-Times* has stood tall with the State of Israel and the Weizmann Institute. This is a legacy that will never, never change." **David Radler, publisher of the *Chicago Sun-Times* and the *Jerusalem Post*** [74]

Hollinger became the target of criminal and civil indictments for massive corruption. In May of 2004, after Conrad Black was ousted, Hollinger International filed a $1.25-billion racketeering suit against Black and a group of corporate insiders. The suit accused Black and others of misappropriating more than $400 million. When a judge dismissed their racketeering-influenced corrupt practice (RICO) claims, the plaintiffs removed the racketeering claim and refiled the lawsuit, adding former company director Richard Perle as a defendant.

On November 15, 2004, the US Securities and Exchange Commission (SEC) filed a civil fraud lawsuit against Black and Radler, alleging that they cheated and defrauded investors and filed misleading public documents. The SEC suit also alleged that Black and Radler looted $85 million from company coffers for their own use.[75] Criminal indictments soon followed. Federal prosecutors charged Black with eight counts of mail and wire fraud in November of 2005. Conrad Black was accused of diverting $51.8 million of Hollinger shareholder money to himself and associates. While Black maintained his innocence, video surveillance cameras captured footage of the former CEO and associates removing boxes of subpoenaed evidence from Hollinger headquarters in Montreal on May 25, 2005 in violation of Canadian and US court orders.[76] The *Chicago Sun-Times* loyally went to press with story about the innocence of Black's removal of the "thirteen boxes":

> "The charges include obstruction of justice for allegedly removing documents from his Toronto office last year. At a court hearing Friday, prosecutors said they wanted to make sure the evidence stayed out of Black's reach. But a lawyer for Black said the material includes items with no relevance to the case, including a picture of Black's father.
>
> After the hearing, Black said the items also include a bust of Marshal Ferdinand Foch—a French military commander from World War I—and a sketch of Maurice Duplessis, who served as premier of Quebec from 1936 to 1959. Black is the author of a 1976 biography of Duplessis.
>
> 'There's a lot of nonsense going on here. This has absolutely no relevance to this case,' Black said. 'It's irritating. Come on, it would be irritating to you, wouldn't it? If you had pictures of your family, a picture of the guy you wrote a book about that his secretary gave you, that had been a present from his own parliamentary caucus?'
>
> Black's interest in historical figures like Foch dates back to his childhood, when he was fascinated with Napoleon. In 2003 he published a second work of history, the 1,360-page *Franklin Delano Roosevelt:*

*Champion of Freedom."* **Eric Herman, *Chicago Sun-Times*, 2/11/2006** [77]

Although the Hollinger directors are innocent until proven guilty, Hollinger's criminal operation is a microcosm of how neoconservative power functions in the media. Not only did Hollinger provide Black with illicit wealth and editorial power over major print media in the US and the rest of the world, but those illicit proceeds sustained payola for neoconservative pundits and ideas that would never have reached a mass audience without Black's largesse.

# *Payola for Pundits*

Conrad Black formed a Hollinger "advisory board" that paid neocon luminaries such as Richard Perle and columnist George F. Will $25,000 per day to "discuss ideas." George Will, a columnist for the Washington Post Writers Group, returned the favor to Black by promoting his views on the need to invade Iraq amid the clutter of ill-informed "opposition" in his March 4, 2003 column:

> "Into this welter of foolishness has waded Conrad Black, a British citizen and member of the House of Lords who is a proprietor of many newspapers, including the Telegraph of London and the Sun-Times of Chicago." [78] **George Will**

None of Will's columns ever revealed his financial relationship with Black and Hollinger. When later queried about the Hollinger $25,000 payments, George Will confessed that he did not recall how many times he'd received them, though others attending the same meetings received up to $200,000 over a number of years.

Richard Perle's enjoyment of Hollinger's large illicit payments did not end with advisory and Board of Directors compensation. Hollinger International, like Boeing, invested $2.5 million in Richard Perle's venture capital fund, Trireme Venture Partners LLP. A civil suit filed on behalf of Hollinger shareholders seeking $5.4 million from Richard

Perle revealed the amount of compensation Perle received through various roles at Hollinger.

The Hollinger shareholders' lawsuit accused Perle, along with Conrad Black and David Radler, of looting Hollinger of hundreds of millions of dollars. The core of the suit accuses Perle of failing to protect shareholders as a board member. When Perle joined Hollinger in 1994, he was paid $250,000 as well as a $50,000 annual bonus to head a subsidiary, Hollinger Digital, that invested in Internet companies. Perle then arranged to receive an additional $3.1 million in "incentive payments" from the subsidiary.

The lawsuit accused Perle of quid pro quo corruption and conflicts of interest.

> "Because he was receiving millions of dollars in compensation from Hollinger at Black's and Radler's discretion, Perle had a motive to rubber-stamp transactions Black and Radler proposed, and Perle did so, despite his duty to Hollinger's shareholders." **Lawsuit Filing**[79]

The suit alleges that Perle improperly approved a loan to Black's holding company. He later approved a reduction of the interest rate on a loan, as well as signing off on a raft of transactions through which Black and Radler allegedly illegally enriched themselves at the expense of shareholders.

Even without the payola, Conrad Black's promotion of Richard Perle, George Will, and William Safire's neocon talking points in the *Chicago Sun-Times*, *Jerusalem Post*, and *Daily Telegraph* allowed them *entrée* to endless cable shows and "expert" interviews.

Black was not the only media mogul with a soft spot and open wallet for neocons. Rupert Murdoch, chairman and chief executive officer of News Corporation and Fox News, financially supported William Kristol and David Brooks's loss leader *The Weekly Standard* and endless neocon media appearances on Fox News programs. Committed to core neoconservative dogma, Murdoch was quoted in the magazine *15 Minutes* telling of a trip in which he took a group of editors from New York and London to spend a weekend at Ariel Sharon's ranch. Aboard a helicopter gunship, the group flew over the Golan Heights, West Bank, and illegal settlements.

> "We saw the vulnerability of the country. Not all New York newspapers feel the cause of Israel is all the news that's fit to print." **Rupert Murdoch**[80]

Other publishers were well aware of the neoconservative media presence. A glimpse at Gaffney's propaganda operation is revealing; in the mid-1990s, Gaffney was routinely faxing 1,000 national reporters, policymakers, and talk radio hosts with two or three talking point papers and reactions per week. His perspectives and pushes for spiraling military spending were always positioned as those of a "defense institute analyst" rather than a paid industry lobbyist.

> "Frank is the conservatives' rapid deployment force for national security." **Robert Andrews, chief Washington lobbyist for Rockwell International Corp.**[81]

News media at all levels swallowed Gaffney's free and polished content on defense and foreign issues, offering little opportunity for counterpoints or critical analysis. Gaffney's weekly, but influential column in the tiny *Washington Times* was supplemented by regular appearances on talk radio shows and even his own weekly thirty-minute television show, which ran for a year.

The massive distribution of Gaffney content shows that the commercial media is structurally more accommodating to a pro-military-spending point of view, even if it distorts and limits public debate. This is entirely understandable. Few newspapers in this era of declining subscription and viewership levels are willing to present an editorial or news environment that is unfriendly to $25,000 two-page Boeing or Lockheed Martin ads. Nevertheless, the relative absence of debate strongly favors repeated content from a few neocon military contractor brokers.

> "(Gaffney's ubiquity) conveys the perception that he represents more people than he really does. He actually represents a very small segment of public opinion." **Jack Mendelsohn, deputy director of the Arms Control Association**[82]

Gaffney's media success is not a solo performance. Neoconservatives are an unavoidable news media presence, placed in all strategic outlets from the *NewsHour with Jim Lehrer* to the *Los Angeles Times* editorial page. But this is testimony to behind-the-scenes money, influence, and media savvy, rather than the inherent strength of their arguments.

Quite simply, neoconservative thought, distributed by think tanks such as the American Enterprise Institute and Heritage Foundation, is better funded and consequently enjoys broader media distribution than any other school of thought in the United States. And in the US, there is no substitute for mainstream media distribution.

The US news media has been uniquely accommodating to neoconservative viewpoints and ideas. Strong editorial control is one reason that so few critical editorials or exposés ever appear in mainstream news publications. The reaction of Mortimer Zuckerman of *US News and World Report* (a former chair of the Conference of Presidents of Major Jewish Organizations) to a rare article about divestment in the Davos-Economic-Forum-sponsored *Global Agenda* magazine is illustrative. The article, by Palestinian activist and Yale professor Mazin Qumsiyeh, recommended divestment from Israel as a way to pressure it to adopt better human rights policies. Qumsiyeh's views about US international relations are *de facto* banned in the US mainstream corporate and public media, which has already decided that they are dangerous and not as potentially lucrative as Gaffney's. Qumsiyeh's writing will certainly never draw a two-page Lockheed Martin spread.

Accountability has also been banished as a relevant factor for news source evaluation in corporate mainstream media. At best, neoconservative musings and forecasts about Iraq have been shown to be completely wrong; at worst, growing numbers of readers and viewers consider them to be conscious fabrications.

Nevertheless, the neoconservative hold on key positions in the mainstream corporate news media has not suffered any backlash. David Brooks has not been discredited or asked to step down; nor has William Kristol. They spin as fast as they can, and new theories and explanations for why the US should continue to follow disastrous policies continue to fly from the screen and deplete the national treasury.

## America's Largest Privately Subsidized "News" Sources

The *NewsHour with Jim Lehrer* relies upon corporate and foundation grants, as well as funding from the Corporation for Public Broadcasting. David Brooks, a neoconservative "analyst," appears at least weekly on the show to present neoconservative viewpoints. While the NewsHour's funding is disclosed in the closing credits, Brooks's funding base is not.

## *Dogma #4: Plunder and Saturate Media Networks*

Brooks is another node of the vast neoconservative media outreach network that is privately subsidized and does not disclose sources or amounts of think tank, corporate, private individual, foundation, and consulting funding. However, Brooks and other neoconservatives are presented to viewers and readers as if they were there on their own merit and strength of ideas.

Nothing could be further from the truth.

Without Conrad Black, Rupert Murdoch, and other enablers, the neocon network would never have deeply penetrated the American psyche. The civil and SEC lawsuits may eventually find that Conrad Black's subsidies of neoconservative pundits were paid for by looting the Hollinger company. Neocon analysts are the athlete on steroids elbowing out the competition because of an undisclosed advantage. Worse, by crowding out serious discussion of domestic and foreign policy with their slogans and selective historical references, they make the American people poorly informed and unprepared to act in society or at the polling place. Common sense and open debate have been put on the defensive in the broadcast news media and broadsheets.

# Dogma #5: The Primacy of Israel

"'[The] security of Israel is the key to security of the world.' Rice added that she feels 'a deep bond to Israel.'

Asked if her feelings toward Israel stem from her religious convictions, Dr. Rice said, 'That is a very deep question. I first visited Israel in 2000. I already then felt that I am returning home despite the fact that this was a place I never visited. I have a deep affinity with Israel.'" **Condoleeza Rice, May 13, 2003** [83]

*A priori* devotion to Israel is a common denominator for all neoconservatives. Former Undersecretary of Defense for Policy Douglas Feith and his father Dalck Feith were honored at the Zionist Organization of America (ZOA)'s annual dinner in 1997. Dalck Feith's Zionist credentials are historic. He was a brownshirt militant in the Zionist Betar youth movement founded by pro-Mussolini visionary Ze'ev Jabotinsky, who molded the movement and later the formation of the Likud party.

ZOA described the Feiths as "noted Jewish philanthropists and pro-Israel activists." Dalck received a special Centennial Award "for his lifetime of service to Israel and the Jewish people." Douglas received the lesser, yet "prestigious" Louis D. Brandeis Award.

Feith's career of militant Zionism was supported by ZOA and Israeli military contractors. In 1999, ZOA published Feith's essay in a book titled *The Dangers of a Palestinian State*. Feith delivered an exhortation demanding "U.S. action against Palestinian Arab killers of Americans" and relocating the U.S.

embassy from Tel Aviv to Jerusalem in 1999. When Douglas Feith left a DOD job in mid-1986, he founded an Israel-based law firm with a client list that included US military contractor Northrop Grumman. Feith's Washington, DC law firm formed an alliance with the Israel-based Zell, Goldberg & Co., a partnership branded the Fandz International Law Group. After the US invasion of Iraq, Feith and Zell attempted to broker Iraq reconstruction contracts, announcing that their group [84]

> "has recently established a task force dealing with issues and opportunities relating to the recently ended war with Iraq, and is assisting regional construction and logistics firms to collaborate with contractors from the United States and other coalition countries in implementing infrastructure and other reconstruction projects in Iraq." **Feith and Zell**[85]

Although Feith's militant Zionism is evident after even a cursory review of his writings, he frequently publicly denied his contributions to the cause. When challenged about his co-authorship of the consulting report for Benjamin Netanyahu, "A Clean Break" (see appendix), Feith denied responsibility via a letter to the editor of the *Washington Post*:

> "There is no warrant for attributing any particular idea [in the Clean Break Plan], let alone all of them, to any one participant." **Douglas Feith**[86]

After entering the Pentagon as an undersecretary in July of 2001, Feith would no longer answer any journalists' questions about policy directives in his articles and speeches. Al Ahram reporter Khaled Dawoud asked Feith point-blank if he still believed, as he had previously written, that "Jordan is Palestine." Feith refused to answer.

What are the roles of Judaism, Zionism, and Israel in the neoconservative movement? Few choose to write about or publicly debate the issue, which is allegedly "toxic" to polite consideration. *Slate Magazine* editor Michael Kinsley once grappled with the issue of the predominant religion of Bush's war advisors.

## *Dogma #5: The Primacy of Israel*

"The lack of public discussion about the role of Israel in the thinking of President Bush is easier to understand, but weird nevertheless. It is the proverbial elephant in the room: Everybody sees it, no one mentions it. The reason is obvious and admirable: Neither supporters nor opponents of a war against Iraq wish to evoke the classic anti-Semitic image of the king's Jewish advisers whispering poison into his ear and betraying the country to foreign interests. But the consequence of this massive "Shhhhhhhh!" is to make a perfectly valid American concern for a democratic ally in a region of nutty theocracies, rotting monarchies, and worse seem furtive and suspicious." **Michael Kinsley, 2002**[87]

The March/April 2004 issue of *Adbusters*, a Vancouver-based, not-for-profit, 120,000-circulation magazine concerned about the "erosion of our physical and cultural environments by commercial forces," brashly weighed in on the issue. *Adbusters* published what it hoped would be a controversial statistic about Kinsley's "elephant." It asked the question, "Why are so many prominent neocons Jewish?" (see full ad in Appendix E).

"Here at Adbusters, we decided to tackle the issue head on and came up with a carefully researched list of who appear to be the 50 most influential neocons in the US [see Appendix E]. Deciding exactly who is a neocon is difficult since some neocons reject the term while others embrace it. Some shape policy from within the White House, while others are more peripheral, exacting influence indirectly as journalists, academics and think tank policy wonks. What they all share is the view that the US is a benevolent hyper power that must protect itself by reshaping the rest of the world into its morally superior image. And half of them are Jewish." *Adbusters* [88]

## Deadly Dogma:
### How Neoconservatives Broke the Law to Deceive America

*Adbusters* was correct that even using the label "neoconservative" to describe this coherent group with highly refined political views has at times generated vehement retaliation, as Middle East envoy Anthony Zinni discovered. Zinni once made a highly critical statement about neocons embedded in the Bush administration policy machine and their Middle East policies in a *Washington Post* interview:

> "'Iraq is in serious danger of coming apart because of lack of planning, underestimating the task and buying into a flawed strategy,' he says. 'The longer we stubbornly resist admitting the mistakes and not altering our approach, the harder it will be to pull this chestnut out of the fire.'...

> The more he listened to Wolfowitz and other administration officials talk about Iraq, the more Zinni became convinced that interventionist 'neoconservative' ideologues were plunging the nation into a war in a part of the world they didn't understand. 'The more I saw, the more I thought that this was the product of the neocons who didn't understand the region and were going to create havoc there. These were dilettantes from Washington think tanks who never had an idea that worked on the ground.'

> 'I don't know where the neocons came from—that wasn't the platform they ran on,' he says. 'Somehow, the neocons captured the president. They captured the vice president.'" **Anthony Zinni, former Chief of Central Command, Middle East**[89]

### *Dogma #5: The Primacy of Israel*

Zinni's criticism of the lack of experience and workable ideas in neocon circles drew an immediate and asymmetrical attack. He was smeared as an "anti-Semite" and "Jew-hater."

> "Discussing the Iraq war with the Washington Post last week, former General Anthony Zinni took the path chosen by so many anti-Semites: he blamed it on the Jews.
>
> Neither President Bush nor Vice-President Cheney—nor for that matter Zinni's old friend, Secretary of State Colin Powell—was to blame. It was the Jews. They 'captured' both Bush and Cheney, and Powell was merely being a 'good soldier.'
>
> Technically, the former head of the Central Command in the Middle East didn't say 'Jews.' He instead used a term that has become a new favorite for anti-Semites: 'neoconservatives.' As the name implies, 'neoconservative' was originally meant to denote someone who is a newcomer to the right. In the 90s, many people self-identified themselves as 'neocons,' but today that term has become synonymous with 'Jews.'" **Joel Mowbray**[90]

This type of smear continues to be a powerful way to deflect or preempt criticism of what are otherwise eminently vulnerable and weak strategic policies. Many "examples" have been made of honest opponents to neocon doctrines through the innuendo of bigotry. If individuals with impeccable military credentials and foreign policy experience can be so easily smeared as "anti-Semites" by thin-skinned defenders of neocon dogma, then no one is safe to criticize them.

In countless speeches, General Zinni would go to great lengths to clarify what he saw as a major problem: "mad mullahs" on all sides of the conflict—Islamic religious fundamentalists abroad, and by implication, evangelicals and other militant Zionists at home.

Some neoconservatives react by watering down any idea of a religious concentration in neocon circles, their interaction and cross-promotion, or even the name "neocon."

> "The full-mooners fixated on a think tank called the Project for the New American Century, which has a staff of five and issues memos on foreign policy. To hear these people describe it, PNAC is sort of a Yiddish Trilateral Commission, the nexus of the sprawling neocon tentacles.
>
> We'd sit around the magazine guffawing at the ludicrous stories that kept sprouting, but belief in shadowy neocon influence has now hardened into common knowledge. Wesley Clark, among others, cannot go a week without bringing it up. In truth, the people labeled neocons (con is short for 'conservative' and neo is short for 'Jewish' ) travel in widely different circles and don't actually have much contact with one another." **David Brooks, 12/30/2003**

*Adbusters* asked why so many neocons are Jewish, since Jews comprise at most 1-2% of the US population. The corollary question is also useful. Why are so many Jews not neoconservative? Why are so many Christians neoconservative, as well as people of indeterminate religious affiliation? One reason may be that the membership requirements to enter the neocon club are actually much stricter than any religious litmus test.

## *Dogma #5: The Primacy of Israel*

A core neoconservative membership requirement is vocal militant Zionism. Neoconservatives are true militants, with a commitment ranging from aggressive action to actual warfare.[91]

Exploring militant Zionism and how it affects neocon thinking is a valuable exercise, particularly for Americans who reject the current path of US Middle East policy and groups that exercise undue influence on its formulation.

Zionism is the ideology that supports a Jewish homeland on land where Jewish kingdoms and self-governing states existed at various times in history. While Zionism is based heavily upon religious tradition linking the Jewish people to the Land of Israel, the modern movement was originally secular, beginning largely as a response to rampant anti-Semitism in late-19th-century Europe.

The Zionist movement only received League of Nations (a precursor to the UN) and British sponsorship after World War I. This resulted in the creation of the British Mandate of Palestine, which stipulated "placing the country under such political, administrative and economic conditions as will secure the establishment of the Jewish national home." The governing Balfour Declaration made promises to secure the interests of all nationalities within the territory:

> "It being clearly understood that nothing shall be done which may prejudice the civil and religious rights of existing non-Jewish communities in Palestine, or the rights and political status enjoyed by Jews in any other country." **Balfour Declaration, 11/2/1917**

After an extremely violent Mandate period marked by terrorism, massacres, and Arab opposition, the state of Israel's founding fathers successfully established the State of Israel in 1948 as a post-Holocaust refuge for the destroyed Jewish society in Europe. Accurate historical accounts of the creation of the state reveal that it was born of terrorism.

> "The reality on the ground was that of an Arab community in a state of terror facing a ruthless Israeli army whose path to victory was paved not only by its exploits against the regular Arab armies, but also by the intimidation and at times atrocities and massacres it perpetrated against the civilian Arab community. A panic-stricken Arab community was uprooted under the impact of massacres that would be carved into the Arabs' monument of grief and hatred." **Shlomo Ben-Ami, former Israeli Foreign Minister under Ehud Barak, 2006**[92]

The neoconservative embrace of Israel, however, is an issue of both faith and, more dangerously, willful self-delusion. It is uncritical to the point of hypocrisy, and has a highly selective memory for facts and history. A case in point is the history of Zionist terrorism. While even high-ranking Israelis are stepping forward to come to grips with Israel's foundation legacy of dispossession and terrorism, no neoconservatives in the United States will publicly acknowledge that the object of their devotion has a checkered past. This is generally not the case for prominent Israelis, who are beginning to lift the lid on the issue.

> "Israel, as a society, also suppressed the memory of its war against the local Palestinians, because it couldn't really come to terms with the fact that it expelled Arabs, committed atrocities against them, and dispossessed them. This was like admitting that the noble Jewish dream of statehood was stained

forever by a major injustice committed against the Palestinians and that the Jewish state was born in sin." **Shlomo Ben-Ami, former Israeli Foreign Minister under Ehud Barak, 2006** [93]

The inability to face up to Israel's history of violence and apply the lessons learned to the present has made neoconservatives an unreliable and particularly dangerous set of advisors on US Middle East policy. In January of 2006, neoconservatives railed against Palestinians and their election of Hamas, a group on the State Department's list of terrorist organizations, to government. The call to isolate and punish the Palestinians, a staple of neocon policy, was immediately broadcast throughout the American news media. Neocons have chosen to forget and will not broach any historical review of Israel's founding fathers' transformation from terrorists into statesmen. "Responsible" editors following the Radler and Zuckerman tradition keep this type of analysis off the news page, replacing it with endless neocon lectures about the consequences of supporting terrorism.

> "Their own people, which is the voters. Now I think our job is to hold the voters accountable, to remind them in a democracy choices have consequences.
>
> You choose Hamas, we understood why you choose it. Nonetheless, we can't deal with a Hamas. We're going to isolate you. In the battle over the next years is the administration saying we can't deal with Hamas, the Israelis saying we can't deal with Hamas, the Palestinians saying in the first sentence we can't deal with Hamas. And in the second sentence but they are making these little gestures, let's deal with them.
>
> And so I think it important to maintain a clear front that we're not going to deal with Hamas because decisions and votes have consequences." **David Brooks, January 2006**[94]

## Deadly Dogma:
### How Neoconservatives Broke the Law to Deceive America

David Brooks, a self-identified neocon analyst who knows his history, is also publicly oblivious about the vital role terrorism played in the formation of Israel and the path this might reveal to other groups wishing to transform from terrorists to statesmen. The motto of one Jewish terrorist group, Lehi, has not been erased by the neocon sands of time:

> "Neither Jewish morality nor Jewish tradition can negate the use of terror as a means of battle." **Lehi motto**[95]

Neoconservative pundits, in a fit of collective historical amnesia, warned that the elections would put the "terror masters" in control of any future Palestinian state, leading to chaos and horror for Israel and the region. This is a clear case of selective amnesia: the transformation from terrorist to statesman constitutes the biographies of many of Israel's founding fathers.

The Lehi Group (short for "Fighters for the Freedom of Israel") was a self-described terrorist group fighting to evict the British from Palestine and form a Jewish state. It later became known as the Stern Gang, after Commander Avraham Stern.

Stern believed that Palestine's Jewish population should fight the British rather than support them in World War II, and even made independent contact with the Nazis, proposing alliance with Germany in exchange for a Jewish state in Palestine.

Lehi assassinated British police and soldiers, and in 1947 conspired to send mail bombs to British politicians in England. Lehi also sabotaged railroads, bridges, and oil refineries in terror operations financed by private donations, bank robbery, and extortion.

## *Dogma #5: The Primacy of Israel*

On November 6, 1944, Lehi assassinated a British government official, Lord Moyne, in Cairo. This murder outraged Winston Churchill, and two captured Lehi assassins were executed. In 1948, Lehi and another Jewish terrorist group, Irgun, attacked the Arab village of Deir Yassin alongside other "irregular" forces in what became known as the Deir Yassin massacre.

Lehi was successfully integrated into the Israeli Defense Forces on May 31, 1948 and Lehi leaders received amnesty from prosecution, although Lehi did later assassinate UN envoy Count Folke Bernadotte in Jerusalem.

Former Israeli Prime Minister Yitzhak Shamir was Lehi's "terror master" when Lehi assassinated Britain's Minister of State for the Middle East, Lord Moyne. Shamir also directed the attempted assassination of Harold Mac Michael, high commissioner of the British Mandate of Palestine, and oversaw the 1948 Bernadotte assassination. Although Bernadotte had secured the release of 21,000 prisoners headed for Nazi extermination, Shamir still judged him to be an agent of Lehi's "British enemy."

Neocons are not on solid historical ground when they insist that Hamas can't follow a similar route of transformation, institutionalization, and legitimization once territorial issues are finalized. The parallels between Lehi and Hamas are haunting: alliances with unsavory foreign countries and an "ends justify the means" approach to violence and terrorism. Hamas, like Lehi, has the popular backing and potential to demand the same amnesty, support, and forgiveness that Lehi ultimately received, not only from a new state, but from the rest of the world. However, neoconservatives refuse to consider history that does not fit their *a priori* belief that Israel can do, and has done, no wrong. The neoconservative view generally augments the corporate mainstream media's self-censorship in four areas:

***Deadly Dogma:***
***How Neoconservatives Broke the Law to Deceive America***

1. Zionist terrorism and violence against the Palestinians in the years before the creation of the state.

2. Whether Israel is viewed as the last Western "colony" forcefully inserted into the region by Arabs and other nationalities.

3. Whether Israeli advocates in the US wield undue influence on regional foreign policy.

4. That Israel is in violation of international laws.

This censorship is extremely useful in a shallow sense to neoconservatives, who win the argument by non-engagement. Winston Churchill may be the intellectual grandfather of the discussion ban and the need for opponents and native peoples of the region to "grin and bear" Israel without complaining about the costs.

> "I'm committed to creation of a Jewish National Home in Palestine. Let us go on with that; and at end of war we shall have plenty of force with which to compel the Arabs to acquiesce in our designs. Don't shirk our duties because of difficulties." **Winston Churchill, July 2, 1943** [96]

The historical record confirms that terrorism against the British and Arab populations in Palestine was ultimately an effective, if horrific, strategy for creating the state of Israel, and that terrorist groups and leaders are part of the nation's foundation legacy. This inconvenient historical fact about Israel is not accepted by neocons. To enter the club, one has to be both a true believer and a forgetter.

# Neocon Membership Requirements

To discover the neocon network's membership requirements, we must empirically ask, "What does it take to become a neoconservative?" Entering or receiving the support of the neocon network seems to have three binding real-world requirements.

One must either have a track record of supporting increasing military funding (since this spending sustains the neocon network), or be silent on the issue and a leading advocate of technical but critical secondary issues, such as rejection of inconvenient international laws (e.g. legal scholar John Yoo). The most important and non-negotiable membership requirement is that one must either be a militant Zionist or indistinguishable from one in word and deed. One must exhibit a committed, *a priori* belief in the state of Israel and have no uncorrected record of criticizing Israeli policies or talking about uncomfortable historical facts. Conservatives such as Pat Buchanan or former Illinois Republican congressman Paul Findley could never redeem themselves from their history of highly critical views of Israel, its origins, and policies. Other politicians, such as Jesse Helms, have had to learn their lessons the hard way in order to stay in power.

At one point, North Carolina Senator Jesse Helms almost lost the confidence of the neocon network and its handmaiden Israeli lobby for opposing exorbitant aid to Israel. Israeli political action committees poured $222,342 into the campaign of Helms's opponent, North Carolina Governor James Hunt. Hunt's campaign secretary proclaimed, "Senator Helms has the worst anti-Israel record in the United States Senate and supporters of Israel throughout the country know it." After the scare of almost losing reelection, Helms announced that he would make U.S. foreign aid to Israel exempt from cuts, since such aid was "in the strategic interest of the U.S." He also became an ardent and comical supporter of moving the US embassy from Tel Aviv to Jerusalem and worked diligently to increase the appropriations for Israel from the Defense Department, the State Department, and half a dozen other different federal agency budgets.[97]

The lingering question about neoconservatives' embrace of Israel is a "chicken or the egg" question. Do neoconservatives have contempt for international law, Arab states, and non-government organizations because they are militant Zionists passionately attached to Israel? Or does their contempt for international law, Arab states, and non-governmental institutions make them gather about Israel as natural allies? Whichever is the cause, neoconservative contempt for international law is another well-documented and defining characteristic of the group.

## *Stifling Debate*

No subject deserves more debate in the United States than its relationship with Israel. No other debate is more actively suppressed, by neoconservatives, editorial gatekeepers and others, in the halls of Congress, the news media, and virtually any other significant channel. George Washington, in his farewell address, warned future generations of Americans about the need for reason, objectivity, and healthy distance to govern American relationships with foreign nations.

> "The government sometimes participates in the national propensity, and adopts through passion what reason would reject; at other times, it makes the animosity of the nation subservient to projects of hostility instigated by pride, ambition, and other sinister and pernicious motives. The peace often, sometimes perhaps the liberty, of nations has been the victim.
>
> So likewise, a passionate attachment of one nation for another produces a variety of evils. Sympathy for the

favorite nation, facilitating the illusion of an imaginary common interest in cases where no real common interest exists, and infusing into one the enmities of the other, betrays the former into a participation in the quarrels and wars of the latter, without adequate inducement or justification. It leads also to concessions to the favorite nation of privileges denied to others, which is apt doubly to injure the nation making the concessions, by unnecessarily parting with what ought to have been retained, and by exciting jealousy, ill-will, and a disposition to retaliate, in the parties from whom equal privileges are withheld. And it gives to ambitious, corrupted, or deluged citizens (who devote themselves to the favorite nation), facility to betray or sacrifice the interests of their own country, without odium, sometimes even with popularity; gilding with the appearances of a virtuous sense of obligation, a commendable deference for public opinion, or a laudable zeal for public good, the base or foolish compliances of ambition, corruption, or infatuation."
**George Washington** [98]

Washington could have been discussing the US relationship with Israel, the largest recipient of American foreign aid, arms, and unconditional political support. However, if a modern-day politician spoke as honestly as Washington, he would quickly face a barrage of neocon charges of anti-Semitism and lack of commitment to national defense.

## *Means Versus Ends*

Brokering military contracts for profit, dominating the news media where possible, and breaking international law (discussed in the next chapter), including espionage on behalf of Israel (final chapter), seem to be merely the *means* to achieve some definite *end*. It is plausible to believe that neoconservative policy is contrived toward one core objective:

advancing what neoconservatives perceive are the interests of Israel.

Neoconservatives are rarely called upon to explain their connections to Israel publicly, and when they are, the answers are usually not very revealing.

> "Brian Lamb: Is this [the invasion of Iraq] a Zionist plot?
>
> Richard Perle: No, of course it isn't a Zionist plot. Of course it isn't. And in fact, prior to the removal of Saddam, if you listened only to what Israelis thought, they thought we were going to the wrong place. At least a lot of Israelis in key positions did. They felt we should go after Iran, that Iran posed a more serious and a more immediate threat. So it wasn't even Israeli policy, for those people who want to suggest that we were simply following Israeli policy. Dismissing my views and David's and others as motivated not by what we say our motives are, but by some hidden motivation, which is somehow to advance the interests of Israel, is a way of avoiding the argument, in my view. Because once you say that, there's not much left to debate.
>
> Brian Lamb: Well, how important is Israel and its future to you personally?
>
> Richard Perle: Israel is a democracy. It is one that I admire. It is in a very difficult situation now that we desperately like to find a way to resolve. It's a country whose destruction, I think, would be a tragedy, not only for Israelis but for the whole world. So I have great sympathy for the plight of the Israelis, which does not and need not come at the expense of sympathy for the plight of Palestinians, who are rather badly governed." **Book Notes interview, 3/7/2004**[99]

## *Dogma #5: The Primacy of Israel*

Pat Buchanan, author of the book *Where the Right Went Wrong*, made a wry observation about the lack of other tenets at the core of neoconservatism as he reviewed an essay by neoconservative Max Boot in the *Wall Street Journal*:

> "In that same Wall Street Journal essay 'What the Heck is a Neocon?' Boot called support for Israel 'a key tenet of neoconservatism.' It was the only tenet Boot mentioned." **Pat Buchanan**[100]

The neoconservative support for Israel is also the only possible explanation for why so many neoconservatives have risked violating US criminal law concerning espionage by passing classified documents to Israel. It also explains why the most committed are repeatedly insinuating themselves into Department of Defense positions, often after losing security clearances over espionage incidents, with the aid of other dedicated neoconservatives (see the final chapter).

# Dogma #6: International Law Is Non-Binding

"I think in this case international law stood in the way of doing the right thing….international law... would have required us to leave Saddam Hussein alone." **Richard Perle, November 19, 2004** [101]

"Our view is that international law is just a part of international politics. States act in their interests and they enter into treaties and other international legal institutions when doing so serves their interests. On this view there is no reason for the U.S. to enter the Kyoto Treaty if as the U.S. government has claimed it puts too much of a burden on the United States relative to other countries. There is no reason to enter the ICC, the International Criminal Court, if the benefits from having this international court are less than the dangers to the United States which are conventionally said to be the risks to American soldiers and leaders being prosecuted for political motives." **Eric Posner, University of Chicago, March 30, 2005** [102]

After World War II, the establishment of strong international institutions allowed the United States to make its case in forums governed by international law and global interests. While the US did not always prevail, respect for the rule of law and general worldwide compliance with useful and verifiable treaties (such as the Non-Proliferation, Law of the Sea, and Anti-Ballistic Missile Treaties and the Geneva Conventions) moved civilization forward.

## Deadly Dogma:
## How Neoconservatives Broke the Law to Deceive America

Neoconservative doctrine rejects the legitimacy and even the existence of international law. In the formal neocon worldview, since international law has no real enforcement mechanisms other than war against transgression or binding mutual interest, international laws are merely expressions of "strong state interests."

> "None of the international organizations that exist today could pass for accountable law-giving, law-interpreting, or law-enforcing bodies....while treaties may well be politically or even morally binding, they are not legally obligatory. They are just not 'law' as we apprehend the term. And what happens to countries when they do not adhere to international law on some matter? Usually nothing. Why, then, do we continue to talk about international 'law'? Because the word has a strong emotive appeal." **John Bolton, January 1, 2000**[103]

Neoconservative zeal for advancing the "no such thing as international law" movement has systematically chipped away at two centuries of growing respect for the rule of law, both inside and outside the United States. Increasing numbers of legal scholars are now reflecting on the potential for abuse that the self-granted neoconservative license to disregard international law advanced by AEI luminaries like John Yoo has created:

> "I strongly believe that state interests can be manipulated by political opportunism, ideological zeal, a misreading of treaties and rules, misreading of facts and of events, and that international law stands in somewhat the same position as constitutional or legislative protection of minority rights: it stands as a check on the abuse of state interests and thus protects the individual, particularly regarding his rights. I would bring that entire argument forward if we were to have a discussion about the detainee abuse scandal. Third, what I believe is a more accurate representation of what we need to consider in

examining international law is not only a threat of state interests, but also a theory of what I call global interests, and I distinguish between this country's state interests and this country's global interests. Global interests is not the same as moral obligation or even the cosmopolitanism theory that is in the book. State interests is only explained by domestic needs and preferences, but global interests in my view comprises both needs and advantages. The needs are we need the world and the world needs us, commercially in our trading, diplomatically in our humanitarian relationships, culturally, even in tourism. Then finally, militarily our global interests projects us far, far beyond our borders in any convenient argument about state interests. It's a proactive view of international law quite distinct from what I would argue with all due respect is a very defensive, intimidated and insecure view of international law." **David Scheffer, George Washington University School of Law** [104]

Neocon reinterpretation of international law has made the United States a rogue state and scofflaw in the eyes of the world. No longer is the US a shining example to be followed in terms of human rights, global environmental protection, non-proliferation, arms control, or any other global interest achievable through restraint and compliance—not with its own private gulag of secret prisons, practice of rendering suspected terrorists to foreign countries for torture, and legal arguments justifying the use of torture in interrogations. These new developments in "misreading of treaties and rules" turning the US into a new Soviet Union are all neoconservative initiatives founded on the concept that international law is a fiction.

In the Senate confirmation hearings for Supreme Court nominee Samuel Alito, executive authority and respect for US law were major issues as neoconservatives successfully began waging war on the idea of restraining the power of the executive.

## Deadly Dogma:
### How Neoconservatives Broke the Law to Deceive America

Neoconservative efforts to unfetter the US from international laws began because they were felt to be limiting the potential revenues of military contractors. Efforts to overturn or thwart treaties began to build as contractors pushed harder for anti-ballistic missile defense projects in the mid-1990s. Treaties stood in the way of commissions.

The neocon American Enterprise Institute was opposed to the intermediate-range nuclear forces treaty that the United States signed in 1988. A special AEI task force fought to refine and deploy Richard Perle's arguments to defeat the measure.

Missile defense lucre motivated the Center for Security Policy and its network to oppose restrictions in the 1972 Anti-Ballistic Missile (ABM) Treaty banning testing and deployment of space weapons systems. The neocon network fought hard to get the administration to suspend ABM treaty negotiations with Russia and other former Soviet states and won the moral support of then-Speaker Newt Gingrich, R-GA. and 16 other House Republicans. The growing coalition asked that negotiations on technical details in the treaty be suspended and delayed, making way for "Star Wars" projects.

But even Republicans were upset when Gaffney and CSP singlehandedly tried to lobby the United States out of the ABM treaty entirely by pushing a House vote. Rep. W. Curtis Weldon, R-PA, urged GOP leaders not to cancel the ABM treaty.

Gaffney and CSP also tried to scuttle the Strategic Arms Reduction Talks II (START II) treaty negotiated by the George H. W. Bush administration. START II sought to cut the number of strategic nuclear warheads by 66% from their Cold War levels. Gaffney attacked the treaty, intensely lobbying the bill when it reached the House and trying to paint Senator Dole, a supporter, as pandering to the Clinton administration:

> "[START II is] one of the most radical disarmament agreements ever to be presented for the Senate's

advice and consent. Is it the spirit of Christmas that prompts Sen. Dole to make such generous presents to his opponents?" **Frank Gaffney, 1995**[105]

# Canceling the Chemical Weapons Convention for Profit

The CSP also tried to broaden the base of anti-treaty proponents in corporate America by quantifying the opportunity cost of the Chemical Weapons Convention. In a grotesque and even ghoulish calculation at a CSP forum, Gaffney reached out to pharmaceutical makers who would lose revenue on vaccine and antidote stockpiles and chemical companies that would suffer "adverse implications" if the government no longer stockpiled chemical weapons under an international ban. Gaffney thought his targets were well picked. He believed the chemical and pharmaceutical industries would surely be able to pay him an appropriate "thank you" sum as military contractors in return for boosting industry revenues.

Despite the best efforts of Gaffney and other neoconservatives to kill the Chemical Weapons Convention, the affected industries were not as shortsighted as Gaffney first believed. The Chemical Manufacturers Association and leading corporations saw their industry benefiting from a chemical-WMD-free world and chose not to cash in on the short-term profits from yet another neocon-induced mini-arms race.

This rebuke of the neocon pitch for a more dangerous world in exchange for short-term industry profits was sensible, but not broad enough. As increasing percentages of US economic production are relegated to military endeavors, the country's consumer product innovation and educational leadership may suffer. Each additional point of GDP devoted to the military is an irreplaceable resource dedicated to the dividends of fear instead of a new generation of wealth creation.

# International Extortion

Richard Perle has gone overseas to ply his unique brand of extortion. In January 2003, Iran/Contra weapons broker Adnan Khashoggi arranged a meeting in France between Harb Saleh al-Zuhair and Richard N. Perle, who was then the acting chairman of the Pentagon Defense Policy Board.

Harb Saleh al-Zuhair was a Saudi industrialist managing investments in construction, electronics, and engineering companies throughout the Middle East. Perle had pitched al-Zuhair to invest in Trireme Venture Partners, LLP with a formal proposal letter. The hook was that Trireme's main business focus on "homeland security," military equipment, and services would benefit from increased demand for such products and services in Europe and countries like Saudi Arabia.[106] Having formed his company two months after 9/11, Perle was clearly seeking to both create and ride an anticipated wave of international terrorism fear. However, Adnan Khashoggi saw Perle mainly as another neocon US government official with a history of "Saudi bashing" seeking to cash in on his influence.

> "It was normal for us to see Perle. We in the Middle East are accustomed to politicians who use their offices for whatever business they want." **Adnan Khashoggi**[107]

Khashoggi's perceptions were buttressed by the proposal letter's reference to Trireme's board:

"Three of Trireme's Management Group members currently advise the U.S. Secretary of Defense by serving on the U.S. Defense Policy Board, and one of Trireme's principals, Richard Perle, is chairman of that Board." **Trireme proposal letter**[108]

The two other Policy Board members Trireme referenced were Henry Kissinger (Nixon's secretary of state), and Gerald Hillman. At that point, Trireme had raised relatively paltry sums for an Internet-bubble-age venture capital fund, including $2.5 million from Conrad Black's Hollinger International and $20 million from Boeing. Gerald Hillman had earlier received $14 million from Hollinger, channeled by then-managing-director Richard Perle into an entity called Hillman Capital. This cash was probably then invested in Trireme to get the total funds under management listed in the proposal letter up to around $45 million.

Gerald Hillman displayed his own credentials rejecting international law during his tenure on the Defense Policy Board in the February 27-28, 2003 meetings. Hillman questioned the validity of Iraq's existing oil contracts with Russia, France, and other nations, advising that the contracts were "bad news" and that the Russians and French should be "kicked out," enabling the US to become the exclusive brokers of Iraqi oil.

Richard Perle had criticized the Saudis and even hosted Defense Policy Board meetings recommending strategies for overthrowing the ruling family and securing the oil fields. Laurent Murawiec, a Rand Corporation analyst, delivered a presentation on why the Saudi regime was a threat to the US.

Kissinger had a thirty-year-old history of fomenting invasion of Saudi Arabia. In 1975, *Harper's Magazine* published a lengthy article titled "Seizing Arab Oil" by a Pentagon analyst using the pseudonym "Miles Ignotus" (unknown soldier), emphasizing the need for the US to seize Saudi oilfields, installations, and airports. According to James Akins, a former US diplomat, the author was probably Henry Kissinger, Secretary of State at the time. Kissinger never confirmed or denied the charge.[109]

The extortion aspects of Richard Perle's calling the meeting were very clear to the Saudi government:

> "Here he is [Perle], on the one hand, trying to make a hundred-million-dollar deal, and, on the other hand, there were elements of the appearance of blackmail— 'If we get in business, he'll back off on Saudi Arabia'—as I have been informed by participants in the meeting." **Saudi Ambassador Bandar Bin Sultan**[110]

The Saudis never invested in Trireme—but the broadly reported incident of attempted blackmail and other shenanigans cost Perle his chairmanship on the Defense Policy Board, and he was later forced to resign from the board entirely.

## Charitable Lawbreaking

The Center for Security Policy, American Enterprise Institute, Project for the New American Century, and Jewish Institute for National Securities Affairs must tread a legal line between military contractors, lobbyists, and IRS rules governing the activities of tax-exempt organizations. The IRS-approved nonprofit mandate of a tax-exempt organization is often very different from how the organization is actually spending money.

The New Citizenship Project (NCP) is the umbrella group for the Project for the New American Century. NCP stated its mission in a 2001 tax filing:

> "Educate in connection with efforts to advance a renewal of American institutions and greater citizen control over national life through publications and other published materials." **New Citizenship Project**[111]

The PNAC website states the objectives of the organization:

> "The Project for the New American Century (PNAC) intends, through issue briefs, research papers, advocacy journalism, conferences, and seminars, to explain what American world leadership entails. It will also strive to rally support for a vigorous and principled policy of American international involvement and to stimulate useful public debate on foreign and defense policy and America's role in the world." **PNAC website**[112]

Yet, in spite of PNAC's nonprofit educational tax-exempt status, the organization directly published no studies or information in 2001. Only $2,942 was spent on 2001 program publications, out of direct public support of $770,000. Total expense for public education events and conferences in 2000 was actually zero.

## Deadly Dogma:
### How Neoconservatives Broke the Law to Deceive America

On September 12, 2003, the PNAC website had only four publications available, two from 2000 and two from 2003. The most famous PNAC publication, "Rebuilding America's Defenses" (September 2000), though of great public interest, was temporarily removed from the NCP website in the months before the Iraq war.

NCP has clearly engaged in lobbying of the Congress and executive branch on behalf of legislation and specific policy initiatives. On January 2, 1998, two NCP directors, William Kristol and Robert Kagan, wrote a letter lobbying then-President Clinton on behalf of NCP (see Appendix C). William Kristol has been commonly seen on Fox News and other channels, raising grassroots support for political causes. Yet for all the political activities and lobbying in its programs, NCP admits neither lobby activities nor expenses on Form 990, line 85b. [113]

The New Citizenship Project may actually be subsidizing a for-profit corporation, the *Weekly Standard*. William Kristol, Chairman of NCP, is also editor of the *Weekly Standard* (TWS), a magazine owned by Rupert Murdoch that promotes the core strategies and policy initiatives of NCP in essay format. TWS was formed by Kristol on September 17, 1995. Other NCP/PNAC/AEI staff and board members, including Robert Kagan, Thomas Donnelly, and Reuel Marc Gerecht, contribute to the policy essays of the *Weekly Standard*, even though NCP does not reveal this close non-exempt relation "through common officers" on line 80 of the 2001 Form 990 (a filing required of tax-exempt nonprofit corporations) as it is legally required to do. Although this magazine is distributed free of charge to the White House and those considered to be "key" policymakers, members of the American public who are interested in NCP and PNAC policy and subsidize it through a tax exemption must buy the magazine at a cost of $48 per year or $3.95 per issue. This operational structure essentially sets up a quid pro quo in which NCP/PNAC serves as a nonprofit, tax-advantaged research house for a for-profit venture, TWS, which then distributes research and policy ideas on behalf of the three foundations that support NCP. TWS earns income from subscription sales while NCP reports no Form 990, line 10a or 10c profit or loss from publications and subscription sales.

In theory, neoconservatives tout the idea that international law does not exist. In practice, they not only break the law themselves, but provide ideological support for laundering, arms trafficking, and more serious charitable fraud from the United States.

# Overseas Charitable Laundering, Fraud, and Ethnic Cleansing

Laundering charitable contributions raised in the US to commit violence and occupation overseas is a direct result of neoconservative ideology at work. An illicit network connects illegal settlements in Israeli-occupied territory, US lobbyists, and charitable entities based in the US and abroad.

Israeli government officials disclosed in August of 2005 that at least US$60 billion has been spent financing illegal settlements in the occupied West Bank and Gaza.[114] According to Israeli prosecutor Talia Sasson, the Israeli government has systematically violated its own laws by financing settlements from foreign donations, the official state budget, and secret military accounts.[115] One global nonprofit, the World Zionist Organization, played a central role in coordinating illegal settlement activities.

Opaque and fungible assets freed up by massive yearly US foreign aid to Israel were poured into settlement development and infrastructure building designed to partition key Palestinian territories and annex others to the state of Israel. US nonprofits were and are directly and indirectly financing the coordination of illegal settlement building, encroachment, and violence against Palestinians. The recently disclosed charitable contributions from neoconservative bagman Jack Abramoff that were laundered to finance violent armed Israeli activity in the Palestinian territories are only the tip of the iceberg. Combining this with the findings of a groundbreaking new study on the causes of suicide terrorism poses a disturbing question: "Are tax-exempt donations from the US causing terrorist retaliation against America?"

## Tax-Exempt Donation Laundering and Terrorism Against the US
*(Source: IRmep – October, 2005)*

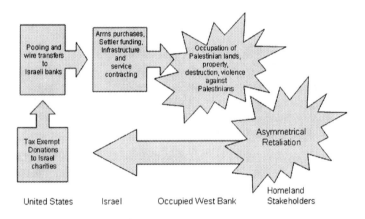

# Money Laundering, Occupation, and Terrorism

Robert Pape's quantitative analysis of terrorist attacks from 1980 to 2003 reveals an uncomfortable truth about the root causes of suicide terrorism: It is a strategic effort to compel target governments to withdraw forces from land that the so-called terrorists perceive as their national homeland. [116] Donations to tax-exempt entities in the US that are laundered and used to kill and maim Palestinians while ethnically cleansing them from their homelands are not cost-free to Americans. This encroachment generates asymmetrical retaliation against soft targets in the US from ideological stakeholders, as referenced in the 9/11 Commission Report.

Americans made $136 billion in tax-deductible charitable contributions in 2002.[117] A significant number of these contributions were aggregated by the network of tax-exempt charities operating on behalf of Israel in the United States and either transferred to finance illegal settlements or used to fund organizations breaking US, Israeli, and international law. Tracing a single $25,000 donation within this enormous flow illuminates the important role of money laundering.

Washington lobbyist Jack Abramoff laundered money from the Choctaw Chippewa Indian tribe into a nondescript 501 (c) (3) called the Capital Athletic Foundation (CAF). In addition to funding the illegal West Bank Beitar Illit colony, CAF directly procured sniper scopes, camouflage suits, night-vision binoculars, a thermal imager, and shooting mats so that Israeli settlers could intimidate or shoot Palestinian Arabs moving through newly captured land. The shipment of military hardware from the US to Israel was to be expedited via signed letter from a commander in the Israeli Defense Force (IDF) in order to guarantee "end user" clearance for arms exportation from the U.S. State Department.[118]

## Tax-Exempt Donation Laundering for Beitar Illit Arms Purchases
*(Source: IRmep 2005)* [119]

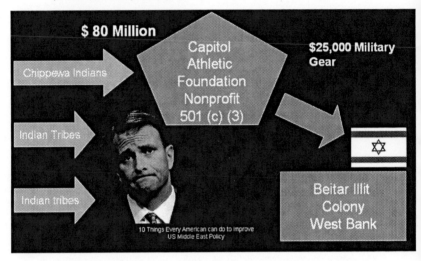

Not all illegal settlement funding from the US is the product of money laundering. A large number of organizations openly raise and disburse funds for the Israeli colonization of Palestinian territories. Although most misrepresent their activities to the IRS as "educational," others, such as the One Israel Fund, Inc. of Cedarhurst, openly tout their efforts to transfer, arm, and promote Jewish settlements in occupied territories.

# US Tax-Exempt Donors to Illegal Settlements
**(Source: Internal Revenue Service)**

| US Tax-Exempt Organization | Tax-Exempt Mandate | Activity |
| --- | --- | --- |
| Christian Friends of Israel (Colorado Springs, CO) | "Educating Christians about the Land of Israel and Biblical significance of current events in the Middle East" | Disbursed $100,061 to an affiliate operating in the West Bank for construction of bus stops, playground equipment in illegal settlements during the year 2003. |
| American Friends of the College of Judea and Samaria (Brooklyn, NY) | "To provide support for the expansion and furtherance of the needs of educational institutions in Israel." | Disbursed $228,200 to an Israeli college established in the illegal West Bank settlement of Ariel. |
| One Israel Fund, Inc. (Cedarhurst, NY) | "The mission of One Israel Fund is to provide essential humanitarian assistance to the over 225,000 men, women, and children living in the 150-plus communities throughout Judea, Samaria, and Gaza (YESHA)." | Disbursed $1.9 million in year 2003 to finance illegal settlements, arms, "Friends of the IDF" organization, and "security equipment." |

Although not all charitable donations to Israel are spent on financing illegal colonization and violence, funds not earmarked for arms or land-grab campaigns offset expenses that otherwise would be paid for by the Israeli government, freeing up fungible resources used for encroachment on Palestinian lands. US charitable contributions have also been used to ensure that settlements continue to spread in occupied territories irrespective of Israeli and international laws.

119

# US Nonprofit Involvement in Illegal Settlement Coordination

American nonprofit organizations control 30% of the World Zionist Organization (WZO) through intermediary governing bodies. On March 9, 2005, Talia Sasson, formerly Israel's chief criminal prosecutor, reported that WZO was deeply involved in coordinating confiscation of privately owned Palestinian land, diverting funds to illegal settlement activity, and acting as the central coordinator for settlement financing and expansion. WZO activities documented in the Sasson report violate international and Israeli laws, as well as American laws prohibiting hostilities against territories or people with which the US is at peace.

# US Nonprofit Control of the World Zionist Organization Settlement Division
*(Source: Forward)* [120]

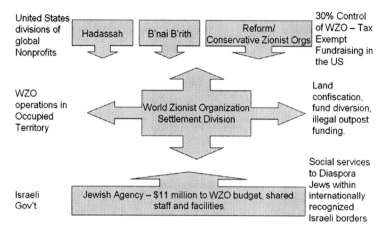

The United States does not escape from the consequences of "charity"-financed ethnic cleansing of the Palestinians. While Palestinians have not struck back at soft US targets in retaliation, "homeland stakeholders" sympathetic to the Palestinian cause, such as 9/11 mastermind Khalid Shaikh Mohammed, have.

> "Yousef's instant notoriety as the mastermind of the 1993 World Trade Center bombing inspired KSM to become involved in planning attacks against the United States. By his own account, KSM's animus toward the United States stemmed not from his experiences there as a student, but rather from his violent disagreement with US foreign policy favoring Israel." **9/11 Commission Report**[121]

The vicious cycle of illegal settlement funding/occupation/retaliation against the US has now become too obvious to deny or explain away. US law enforcement is clearly the best solution for confronting charities operating in the US and laundering tax-exempt donations into illegal settlement activity. To date, however, it is still in an "information gathering" phase and has yet to prosecute any significant neocon overseas criminal activity.

# The Legal Dilemmas of Israel and Terrorism

Neoconservatives undercut and debase the idea of international law because of the implications it has for territorial concessions in the Israeli-Palestinian conflict. This is in direct opposition to the international consensus for a solution to the Palestinian-Israeli conflict based on international law.

> "Since the mid-1970s, there's been an international consensus for resolving the Israel-Palestine conflict. Most of your listeners will be familiar with it. It's called a two-state settlement, and a two-state settlement is pretty straightforward, uncomplicated. Israel has to fully withdraw from the West Bank and Gaza and Jerusalem, in accordance with the fundamental principle of international law, cited three times by Mr. Ben-Ami in the book, his book, that it's inadmissible to acquire territory by war. The West Bank, Gaza and Jerusalem, having been acquired by war, it's inadmissible for Israel to keep them. They have to be returned. On the Palestinian side and also the side of the neighboring Arab states, they have to recognize Israel's right to live in peace and security with its neighbors. That was the quid pro quo: recognition of Israel, Palestinian right to self-determination in the West Bank and Gaza with its capital in Jerusalem. That's the international consensus.

> It's not complicated. It's also not controversial. You
> see it voted on every year in the United Nations. The
> votes typically something like 160 nations on one
> side, the United States, Israel and Naru, Palau,
> Tuvalu, Micronesia and the Marshall Islands on the
> other side. That's it. Now, the Israeli government was
> fully aware that this was the international consensus,
> but they were opposed (a) to a full withdrawal from
> the West Bank and Gaza and Jerusalem, of course,
> and (2) they were opposed to creating a Palestinian
> state in the Occupied Territories." **Norman
> Finkelstein, professor of political science at
> DePaul University, 2006** [122]

Unfortunately, by throwing out the concept of binding
international law, another major neoconservative cause,
international terrorism, is simultaneously undercut. The
neoconservative-coined phrase "global war on terrorism" is
based on the idea that terrorism, unlike traditional warfare, is
an illegal form of violence. In the drive to undercut the
legitimacy of international law, neoconservatives also
undercut the legal basis for their "global war on terror."

# Consequences of Lawbreaking

Few Americans would actually want to live in a world where
international law meant nothing and could be broken on a
whim. Try to imagine making an international phone call, or
better yet, a transatlantic flight, in the total absence of the
plethora of rules that govern telecom protocols, international
standards, air corridors, or protocols for landing in heavily
congested airports.

Neoconservative calls to undermine or ignore international
law are not only foolish and naïve, they also place Americans
in peril. Rejection of the Geneva Convention means that
American POWs will someday face torture at the hands of

their captors. Illicit "extraordinary rendition" means that expeditious and efficient extradition treaties can be replaced by international kidnapping of suspected criminals. In this world, only might makes right.

Neoconservative crimes have largely gone without prosecution. Pursuing an international case about a US government official extorting a Saudi is not high on the DOJ's list of priorities, nor is rolling up charities that finance the neocon dream of a powerful, "greater Israel." The consequence of this failure to uphold the law is clear: increased terrorism against the US over the dying embers of public perception that justice is blind.

# Neocons: America's New Mafia?

The revelations in this book, most of which have appeared in the mainstream press, have caused many to want increased prosecutorial oversight of the neocon network. The neoconservative network has depended on funding, lax law enforcement, and continued cross-promotion of members of the network into positions of influence. Funding flows unabated from military contracts, charities, private donors, and foundations. Some of the funding has been "dirty money," such as corporate monies wrongfully expropriated from Hollinger Corporation and taxpayer revenue from the US Treasury. Some neoconservative activities involve tax fraud and the misuse of charitable organizations.

Neoconservative ideas have wielded power over two elective branches of government, the Executive and Legislative. When neoconservatives have crossed legal lines to obtain power, remuneration and influence, remarkably few criminal prosecutions have been launched by law enforcement and US attorneys.

Resolving documented criminal matters is clearly in the hands of the Department of Justice, a maligned branch of government that has historically been more associated with diminishing American society than restoring it. J. Edgar Hoover, the FBI's battle against civil rights, and the Red Scare continue to haunt the DOJ. However, only the Justice Department has the proper tools and charter to enforce American laws.

The neocons have evolved into a syndicate which, like the Mafia, is difficult to prosecute. Its leadership is readily identifiable, and wherever it goes it leaves a trail of graft, corruption, and lawbreaking. In the case of Middle East policy, there are hundreds of thousands of bodies, but no murder weapon. Every US taxpayer in the station has been pickpocketed, but the neocon train has quietly left the station. Specifics of the neoconservative international extortion and protection rackets are well documented in the news, yet their American leadership has remained untouchable.

Power and influence wielded in concert by neoconservative nonprofits, government officials, and think tanks have led to thirty years of criminal activities.

# *Evolving Prosecutorial Climate*

To date, the DOJ and other law enforcement entities have never prosecuted a policy-driven network as a crime syndicate. Rather, DOJ has prosecuted the most visible and egregious instances of neocon racketeering as isolated crimes perpetrated by individuals. Peripheral crimes are ignored. DOJ is following a long history of US reluctance to prosecute complex crimes perpetrated by prominent members of society.

In response to complaints about criminal coordination of "astroturf" political action committees (PACs), the Federal Election Committee (FEC) found that one extension of the neoconservative movement had "probably" violated the law in the 1990s.[123] But since the target of the legal action was the powerful American Israeli Public Affairs Committee (AIPAC), the FEC and the Supreme Court decided not to take any action.

However, the indictment and guilty plea of Larry Franklin, a former Department of Defense official caught passing classified government documents to AIPAC and Israel, indicates a shift in the prosecutorial climate.

Franklin, a former U.S. Air Force Reserve colonel and U.S. Department of Defense intelligence analyst, pled guilty to passing information to Israel about U.S. policy towards Iran. Judge T. S. Ellis III sentenced Franklin to 151 months in prison and fined him $10,000 on January 20, 2006.

Two top-level AIPAC employees, Kenneth Weissman and Steve Rosen, have also been indicted on charges that they recruited and assisted in Franklin's espionage by passing classified information to Israeli diplomat Naor Gilon. Franklin is expected to testify against Rosen and Weissman.

Many in the Washington establishment have gone public decrying the espionage prosecution and sentencing of Franklin as punishing "freedom of speech."

> "Judge Ellis has it backward. A democratic government does not, in general, 'authorize' the information citizens are allowed. Given enough information, citizens authorize and control their government. Or at least we used to." **Gary Wasserman, Georgetown University**[124]

The AIPAC lobbyists have been compared to news reporters out to inform their constituents who enjoy First Amendment protection.

> "Dr. Rosen, Mr. Weissman, and other foreign policy advocates who, like the press, report to their constituents on the development of policy positions within the government would find themselves speaking on matters of great public concern at the risk of criminal prosecution—undoubtedly resulting in precisely the 'chilling effect' that the First Amendment was intended to avoid." **Abe Lowell and Viet Dihn (PATRIOT ACT author)** [125]

This defense would be plausible in the absence of any long-term pattern of neocon espionage against the United States. Unfortunately for neoconservatives, a clear history of repeated neoconservative espionage and passing classified information to Israel does exist. Their cases differ from the AIPAC spying case only in that they were never prosecuted.

# Espionage

In 1978, Stephen D. Bryen, then a Senate Foreign Relations Committee staffer, was overheard offering "Pentagon documents on the bases" to officials of the Israeli government in a Washington, D.C. restaurant. In 1979, Bryen was observed in his Senate office with Zvi Rafiah, the Mossad (Israeli CIA) station chief in Washington. The two were reviewing and discussing classified documents spread out on a table in front of an open safe. Bryen's fingerprints were found on the classified documents, although he stated in writing to the FBI that the classified material was never in his personal possession. After an investigation, the Justice Department and FBI recommended that Bryen be brought before an investigative grand jury for espionage.

The investigation was shut down. Robert Keuch, the deputy assistant attorney general recommending the grand jury hearing, was denied key documents by the Senate Foreign Relations Committee.

In what has now become an established pattern, the larger neocon network rushed to Bryen's rescue, placing him in yet another sensitive government position with access to classified information. Upon his nomination as assistant secretary of defense for international security, Richard Perle hired Bryen as his deputy assistant secretary. Bryen received Top Secret ("NATO/COSMIC") clearance in April 1981. [126]

In May of 1988, Bryen attempted to approve a license to export four klystrons (advanced radar technology) to Israel on behalf of Varian Associates. At a formal meeting, all US government officials except Bryen opposed the license. Bryen then suggested he would ask the Israelis why they were seeking to buy klystrons. After receiving a *pro forma* response, Bryen approved the export license and the klystrons were released. [127]

Assistant Secretary of Defense Richard Armitage discovered the sale and communicated his objection to the State Department of the Pentagon's official and "uniformly negative" stance on export of klystrons to Israel. The export license was subsequently withdrawn. Varian Associates was then officially banned from contracting with the Defense Department. [128] It was the first company ever banned in this way.

In spite of the controversy and his documented history of breaching national security, Deputy Secretary of Defense Paul Wolfowitz later supported Bryen's accession to the China Commission in April 2001, a term later extended through December of 2005. This placed Bryen in a position to influence US policy regarding Israel's transfer of advanced technology, much of it reverse-engineered from US technology, to China. [129]

In June of 2003, the United States imposed sanctions on Israel after it secretly attempted to sell unmanned aerial vehicles based on US technology to China. In 2000, Israel attempted to sell radar equipment based on US AWACs systems to China in defiance of US export law. [130]

The cross-promotion of members at the top of the neocon network into key US government posts has continued because their history of espionage and security breaches that damage US national security and the confidence of the American people has gone entirely unprosecuted.

Federal law, 18 U.S.C. § 794 (c), makes it a crime to deliver defense information to a foreign government "with intent or reason to believe" that the information will be used in either one of two ways: "to the injury of the United States" or "to the advantage of a foreign nation." With due prosecutorial will and diligence, Richard Perle, Paul Wolfowitz, and Douglas Feith would all have received prison terms and been largely banned from influencing US policy if the documented instances of them violating 18 U.S.C. § 794 (c) had ever been prosecuted. We are left to imagine how law enforcement could have improved US policymaking and cut down on graft. **However, it is still not too late to correct enforcement lapses of the past, particularly the most damaging instances. This is because there is no statute of limitations on espionage.**

# A Short History of Neocon Espionage
*(Source: IRmep 2006)*

| Perpetrator | Incident |
|---|---|
| **Richard Perle** <br> Committee to Maintain a Prudent Defense Policy <br> Staffer to Sen. Jackson <br> Assistant Secretary of Defense <br> Defense Policy Board Advisory Committee <br> Chairman, Defense Policy Board Advisory Committee | Obtained and leaked classified CIA documents on Soviet armaments in 1969. <br><br> In 1975, relayed classified intelligence obtained from Helmut Sonnenfeld on the National Security Council staff through the office of Sen. Jackson to the Israeli embassy. |
| **Paul Wolfowitz** <br> Assistant Secretary of State for East Asian and Pacific Affairs 1982-1986 <br><br> Deputy Secretary of Defense <br> President, World Bank | In 1978, as an employee of the Arms Control and Disarmament Agency, passed classified information through the American Israel Public Affairs Committee to Israel.[131] |
| **Douglas Feith** <br> Middle East Specialist, NSC <br><br> Special Counsel for the Assistant Secretary of Defense for International Security (Richard Perle) <br><br> Undersecretary of Defense for Policy | Fired from the National Security Council for allegations of espionage in and passing classified documents to the Israeli embassy in Washington, DC in 1983.[132] <br><br> Allowed unregistered foreign agents to enter the Pentagon in 2002; divulged classified information.[133] <br><br> Feith's employee Lawrence Franklin convicted of espionage through AIPAC and Israeli diplomats. |
| **Michael Ledeen** <br> American Enterprise Institute | The Pentagon downgraded Ledeen's security clearances from Top Secret- |

| | |
|---|---|
| Hired to the DOD "Office of Special Plans" by Douglas Feith on contract in the year 2001 | SCI to Secret in the mid-1980s after the FBI began a probe of Ledeen for passing classified materials to Israel. Ledeen has been carried in FBI files as an agent of influence of a foreign government: Israel.<br><br>Allegedly also involved in transmission and/or fabrication of the "Niger Forgeries" implicating Iran in the purchase of uranium from Niger.[134] |
| **Stephen Bryen**<br>AIPAC<br>JINSA<br><br>Senate For. Rel. Committee<br>Deputy Under Secretary of Defense from 1981-1988 | After moving from a job at the American Israel Public Affairs Committee to a staff job on the Senate Foreign Relations Committee, was forced to resign after being investigated passing and trying to gain classified information for the Israeli government in 1978.[135] Later brought into the Pentagon by Richard Perle. |
| **Helmut Sonnenfeld** | Transmitted a classified document concerning the commencement of the 1967 "Six-Day War" to an Israeli government official without authorization while serving as a staff member of the State Department's Bureau of Intelligence and Research.<br><br>In 1975, leaked classified data to Richard Perle that Perle later passed on to the Israeli embassy. |
| **Harold Rhode** | In 1998, Rhode had his clearances suspended based on allegations that he had given classified information to Israel. |

Espionage, like treason, is one of the most serious crimes an individual or group of individuals can perpetrate against the United States. The common defense of espionage on behalf of Israel is that it is a "friendly nation." Elements in the mainstream news media has been particularly eager to convey this false interpretation to readers:

> "Now a professor at Georgetown University Law Center, Mr. Dinh joined with lawyers Abbe D. Lowell and John Nassikas in a motion filed in U.S. District Court in Alexandria condemning the charges as 'a dangerous attempt by prosecutors to overextend to private citizens a statute which was intended to apply solely to government officials with access to classified information.'

> The motion said the indictment violated First Amendment protections due a lobbying organization whose policy activity and civic engagement 'is the very justification for a free press and free speech.'

> 'This is what members of the media, members of the Washington policy community, lobbyists and members of congressional staffs do perhaps hundreds of times every day,' the motion said.

> Prosecutors said Franklin arranged for meetings with those to whom he relayed classified information that could have been used 'to the injury of the United States and to the advantage of a foreign nation.' **Jerry Seper, The Washington Times**[136]

In fact, the Espionage Act makes no such distinction, only that classified data be "used to the injury of the United States *or* to the advantage of a foreign nation."

# USC 18 >PART I>CHAPTER 37>Espionage and Censorship

PART I - CRIMES

HEADING

Sec. 794. Gathering or delivering defense information to aid foreign government

STATUTE

(a) Whoever, with intent or reason to believe that it is to be used to the injury of the United States or to the advantage of a foreign nation, communicates, delivers, or transmits, or attempts to communicate, deliver, or transmit, to any foreign government, or to any faction or party or military or naval force within a foreign country, whether recognized or unrecognized by the United States, or to any representative, officer, agent, employee, subject, or citizen thereof, either directly or indirectly, any document, writing, code book, signal book, sketch, photograph, photographic negative, blueprint, plan, map, model, note, instrument, appliance, or information relating to the national defense, shall be punished by death or by imprisonment for any term of years or for life, except that the sentence of death shall not be imposed unless the jury or, if there is no jury, the court, further finds that the offense resulted in the identification by a foreign power (as defined in section 101(a) of the Foreign Intelligence Surveillance Act of 1978) of an individual acting as an agent of the United States and consequently in the death of that individual, or directly concerned nuclear weaponry, military spacecraft or satellites, early warning systems, or other means of defense or retaliation against large-scale attack; war plans;

> communications intelligence or cryptographic information; or any other major weapons system or major element of defense strategy.

The AIPAC prosecution should only be the first step in a serious American effort to put an end to neoconservative criminality. This can begin with the delivery of indictments covering thirty years of espionage. It can continue with the serious investigation of Michael Ledeen (of Iran-Contra scandal fame) for the fabrication of false intelligence introduced into the US intelligence stream before the US invasion.

Ledeen has been linked to the false intelligence through a former employer, Italy's *Panorama Magazine*, which published the Niger forgeries. His contacts and dates of foreign trips contacting entities and persons who fabricated documents implicating Iraq in procuring uranium from Niger have not been satisfactorily explained. Neocon Irving Lewis Libby has been indicted in relation to the "outing" of CIA operative Valerie Plame in retaliation against an envoy who questioned the Niger forgeries. Neoconservative David Addington (listed as the Vice President's counsel in the indictments) is implicated in instructing Irving Lewis Libby to access records of who sent the whistleblowing diplomat to Niger to check the veracity of the forgeries. Americans are now calling on US attorneys to insist that they investigate well-documented cases of espionage. When espionage is the crime, tough law enforcement under the Espionage Act is clearly the only answer.

## *Conspiracy and Wire Fraud*

On June 15, 2003, former General Wesley Clark told news reporter Tim Russert that neocons inside the Bush administration had engaged in a sophisticated propaganda campaign seeking a *de facto* implication of Saddam Hussein in the 9/11 attacks. According to Clark, the broad campaign started on September 11, 2001 as he and others were urged to make public allegations linking Hussein to the attacks on America. Clark disclosed this conspiracy in an interview with Tim Russert:

> CLARK: There was a concerted effort during the fall of 2001, starting immediately after 9/11, to pin 9/11 and the terrorism problem on Saddam Hussein.

> RUSSERT: By who? Who did that?

> CLARK: Well, it came from the White House, it came from people around the White House. It came from all over. I got a call on 9/11. I was on CNN, and I got a call at my home saying, 'You got to say this is connected. This is state-sponsored terrorism. This has to be connected to Saddam Hussein.' I said, 'But— I'm willing to say it, but what's your evidence?' And I never got any evidence. **Transcript**[137]

The disinformation campaign conducted in the United States is well documented. Hours of video footage of leading neoconservatives making unfounded claims about Saddam Hussein are scattered in digital film vaults across America.

Neoconservatives have passed off this campaign as "erroneous intelligence." However, from a legal standpoint, the concerted behind-the-scenes effort to deluge viewers with unfounded propaganda has another name: criminal conspiracy.

## USC 18>PART I >CHAPTER 19 >§ 371
## Conspiracy to commit offense or to defraud United States

> If two or more persons conspire either to commit any offense against the United States, or to defraud the United States, or any agency thereof in any manner or for any purpose, and one or more of such persons do any act to effect the object of the conspiracy, each shall be fined under this title or imprisoned not more than five years, or both.

The medium used to carry out a conspiracy adds another criminal charge. When television and radio are employed in an effort to defraud, it becomes wire fraud.

> 1343. Fraud by wire, radio, or television

> Whoever, having devised or intending to devise any scheme or artifice to defraud, or for obtaining money or property by means of false or fraudulent pretenses, representations, or promises, transmits or causes to be transmitted by means of wire, radio, or television communication in interstate or foreign commerce, any writings, signs, signals, pictures, or sounds for the purpose of executing such scheme or artifice, shall be fined under this title or imprisoned not more than 20 years, or both. If the violation affects a financial institution, such person shall be fined not more than $1,000,000 or imprisoned not more than 30 years, or both.

The operatives rounding up and coordinating public figures like Wesley Clark to make the Saddam-9/11 connection without any evidence did so with criminal intent. Their motivation was to defraud US citizens and the government to enter a war that neocons had crafted over decades of policy papers and secret machinations.

## *Military Contract Fraud*

In 2003, a network of neoconservatives inside and outside government conspired to push through the lease and purchase of Boeing aerial refueling tankers for $24 billion. While Frank Gaffney, Paul Wolfowitz, Richard Perle, and others on the team may have considered it just another failed military contracting boondoggle, the US criminal code has a special law for organized conspiracies to defraud the US government based on false claims.

## USC 18 > PART I > CHAPTER 15 > § 286. Conspiracy to defraud the Government with respect to claims

> Whoever enters into any agreement, combination, or conspiracy to defraud the United States, or any department or agency thereof, by obtaining or aiding to obtain the payment or allowance of any false, fictitious or fraudulent claim, shall be fined under this title or imprisoned not more than ten years, or both.

The Boeing tanker deal was clearly crafted to defraud the government with respect to actual vs. fraudulent specifications, the use of leases rather than outright purchase, and claims that other tanker infrastructure options, including repair and upgrade of the existing fleet, were impossible.

There are also more than thirty years of written testimony, policy papers, op-eds, and broadcast material produced by Paul Wolfowitz, Richard Perle, Douglas Feith, Frank Gaffney, and others showing a similar history of fraudulent claims about military budgets designed to misallocate spending and defraud the US government and taxpayers indirectly through fraudulent military contract brokering.

Richard Perle and Thomas Donnelly were among the prominent members of the neocon network pushing for the Boeing military contract. They were aware that the specifications did not reflect current need, but they took behind-the-scenes bribes to push the deal through anyway. It is now time to prosecute members of the wider promotional network for attempting to defraud the United States.

# Private Correspondence with Foreign Governments

In 1996, Richard Perle, Douglas Feith, and David Wurmser advised Prime Minister Benjamin Netanyahu to reject US Middle East peace initiatives based on territorial concessions, and to broker missile defense contracts for added influence in the US Congress (see their written final product in Appendix C). This private diplomatic venture also lobbied the Israeli government to take actions that directly opposed the stated foreign policies of the US government. This activity violated the US criminal code:

## USC 18 > PART I > CHAPTER 45 > § 953. Private correspondence with foreign governments

> Any citizen of the United States, wherever he may be, who, without authority of the United States, directly or indirectly commences or carries on any correspondence or intercourse with any foreign government or any officer or agent thereof, with intent to influence the measures or conduct of any foreign government or of any officer or agent thereof, in relation to any disputes or controversies with the United States, or to defeat the measures of the United States, shall be fined under this title or imprisoned

not more than three years, or both.

This section shall not abridge the right of a citizen to apply, himself or his agent, to any foreign government or the agents thereof for redress of any injury which he may have sustained from such government or any of its agents or subjects.

This section of the US code is also known as the Logan Act, named after George Logan. In 1798, this friend and purported political supporter of Thomas Jefferson traveled to Paris with no US credentials to negotiate a binding accord with France during a time of diplomatic tension between the US and France. The Logan Act was created to prohibit precisely the type of unofficial overseas maneuvers that neoconservatives routinely engage in.

This unofficial shuttle diplomacy and "consulting" is against the law for good reason. In the case of "A Clean Break," the neoconservatives were instrumental in defeating US-led peace efforts that comprised the president's official foreign policy. Enforcing the Logan Act ensures that American citizens won't be embroiled in wars, conspiracies, and plots hatched by freelancing Americans of dubious loyalty working against US interests overseas.

## Extortion

When Richard Perle met with Iran/Contra weapons broker Adnan Khashoggi and arranged a meeting in France with Harb Saleh al-Zuhair in January of 2003, he was still acting chairman of the Pentagon Defense Policy Board, a government official of the United States. His attempt to extort hundreds of millions of dollars from Saudi investors in exchange for "laying off" the Saudis is not simply a failed international business deal: it is a crime punishable by three years in prison.

## USC 18 > PART I > CHAPTER 41 >§ 872. Extortion by officers or employees of the United States

> Whoever, being an officer, or employee of the United States or any department or agency thereof, or representing himself to be or assuming to act as such, under color or pretense of office or employment commits or attempts an act of extortion, shall be fined under this title or imprisoned not more than three years, or both; but if the amount so extorted or demanded does not exceed $1,000, he shall be fined under this title or imprisoned not more than one year, or both.

Richard Perle, Douglas Feith and Stephen Bryen are examples of the types of people the US government should not place in positions of influence: beholden to foreign and weapons industry interests, continuously attempting to enrich themselves and members of their network with one foot in the door of government and another in private industry, while promoting the careers of fellow compromised individuals. By rigorously prosecuting bribery and extortion cases, the DOJ can achieve the aims and objectives of these laws: sound government.

# Military Expeditions Against a Friendly Nation

Neoconservatives are uniformly hostile to Palestinians' territorial and statehood claims and have a decades-long policy record calling for their relocation, defunding, targeted liquidation, gradual ethnic cleansing, and removal from the international spotlight. This hostility finds neverending ideological support and diffusion in neoconservative hotbeds such as New York's Hudson Institute.

> "[We need to] consider the Jordan Option." **Meyrav Wurmser, 1/9/2006**[138]

The "Jordan Option" is the concept of ethnically cleansing into Jordan all Arab populations still residing within Israel's borders and the occupied West Bank.

The neoconservatives' broader ideological support for gradual ethnic cleansing provides moral support for real "action on the ground": US-based charitable organizations that finance ethnic cleansing and launder charitable funds for weapons.

Prior to 9/11, the US largely ignored charitable contributions flowing through the global financial system. Monitoring became a priority after 9/11 with US Treasury Department initiatives to confront "terrorism financing" through the department's Office of Foreign Assets Control. However, the US has not done enough to stifle a less obvious but critical terrorism generator: Israeli settler violence and illegal seizure of lands that Palestinians consider their homeland. Fortunately, effective avenues for the prosecution of US charities funneling financial and other forms of support to illegal Israeli settlements already exist in the US criminal code.

## USC 18 > CHAPTER 45--FOREIGN RELATIONS > § 960 Expedition against friendly nation

Whoever, within the United States, knowingly begins or sets on foot or provides or prepares a means for or furnishes the money for, or takes part in, any military or naval expedition or enterprise to be carried on from thence against the territory or dominion of any foreign prince or state, or of any colony, district, or people with whom the United States is at peace, shall be fined under this title or imprisoned not more than three years, or both.

The neoconservative conspiracy to displace Palestinians, people of a nation with which the US is not at war, is also illegal.

## USC 18>CHAPTER 45--FOREIGN RELATIONS>§ 956 Conspiracy to kill, kidnap, maim, or injure persons or damage property in a foreign country

(a)(1) Whoever, within the jurisdiction of the United States, conspires with one or more other persons, regardless of where such other person or persons are located, to commit at any place outside the United States an act that would constitute the offense of murder, kidnapping, or maiming if committed in the special maritime and territorial jurisdiction of the United States shall, if any of the conspirators commits an act within the jurisdiction of the United States to effect any object of the conspiracy, be punished as provided in subsection (a)(2).(2) The punishment for an offense under subsection (a)(1) of this section is--(A) imprisonment for any term of years or for life if the offense is conspiracy to murder or kidnap; and

(B) imprisonment for not more than 35 years if the offense is conspiracy to maim.

(b) Whoever, within the jurisdiction of the United States, conspires with one or more persons, regardless of where such other person or persons are located, to damage or destroy specific property situated within a foreign country and belonging to a foreign government or to any political subdivision thereof with which the United States is at peace, or any railroad, canal, bridge, airport, airfield, or other public utility, public conveyance, or public structure, or any religious, educational, or cultural property so situated, shall, if any of the conspirators commits an act within the jurisdiction of the United States to affect any object of the conspiracy, be imprisoned not more than 25 years.

Charities laundering donations from the US can be prosecuted for their direct or indirect role in acts of property damage, confiscation, occupation, and violence against a nation, the Palestinians, with which the US is at peace.

# *Filing False Tax Returns and Charity Fraud*

In the case of the Project for the New American Century and other neoconservative think tanks, failure to file or declare expenses dedicated to lobbying is clearly tax fraud. It is also fraudulent to expend less than 1% of revenue on the declared "core activity" of a nonprofit: in PNAC's case, public education and research.

## USC 26 > SUBTITLE F > CHAPTER 75 > Subchapter A > PART I § 7206. Fraud and false statements (2) Aid or assistance

> Willfully aids or assists in, or procures, counsels, or advises the preparation or presentation under, or in connection with any matter arising under, the internal revenue laws, of a return, affidavit, claim, or other document, which is fraudulent or is false as to any material matter, whether or not such falsity or fraud is with the knowledge or consent of the person authorized or required to present such return, affidavit, claim, or document;

The deeper question for the IRS about AEI, PNAC, CSP, and JINSA is whether they are truly charities or simply stealth lobbies. PNAC's function as a nonprofit research house for the *Weekly Standard* may not be the only obvious case of neoconservative charity fraud. The detailed donor data that would clarify this is available only to the IRS. However, the IRS should take a close look at the Center for Security Policy. CSP operates much more like a military industry lobby than a nonprofit policy research center, especially since its "research" is limited only to promoting higher spending and ever more sophisticated ballistic missile defense, even in the face of ever-changing military threats. While CSP and the others benefit by hiding the origin of their donations, it is also true that if they act like military contractor lobbyists, lobby Congress, and receive donations from military contractors, they are unregistered lobbies, not tax-favored charities.

# Bribery of Public Officials and Conflicts of Interest

Richard Perle was the assistant secretary of defense for international security policy in the Reagan administration from 1981-1987. During his tenure as a public official, Perle recommended that the Army purchase an armaments system from Israeli arms dealers Shlomo Zabludowicz and his son Chaim Zabludowicz. The Zabludowicz company had paid Perle $50,000 in "consulting fees" the very same month he joined the Reagan administration. Perle claimed the payment was for work done before joining the government and that he had informed the Army of this prior consulting work.[139] Perle's long history of abusing government posts as a willing recipient of bribes for personal profit demands prosecution for bribery.

## USC 18 > PART I > CHAPTER 11 §201
## Bribery of public officials and witnesses

(a) For the purpose of this section—

(1) the term "public official" means Member of Congress, Delegate, or Resident Commissioner, either before or after such official has qualified, or an officer or employee or person acting for or on behalf of the United States, or any department, agency or branch of Government thereof, including the District of Columbia, in any official function, under or by

authority of any such department, agency, or branch of Government, or a juror;

(2) the term "person who has been selected to be a public official" means any person who has been nominated or appointed to be a public official, or has been officially informed that such person will be so nominated or appointed; and

(3) the term "official act" means any decision or action on any question, matter, cause, suit, proceeding or controversy, which may at any time be pending, or which may by law be brought before any public official, in such official's official capacity, or in such official's place of trust or profit.

(b) Whoever—

(1) directly or indirectly, corruptly gives, offers or promises anything of value to any public official or person who has been selected to be a public official, or offers or promises any public official or any person who has been selected to be a public official to give anything of value to any other person or entity, with intent—

(A) to influence any official act; or

(B) to influence such public official or person who has been selected to be a public official to commit or aid in committing, or collude in, or allow, any fraud, or make opportunity for the commission of any fraud, on the United States; or

(C) to induce such public official or such person who has been selected to be a public official to do or omit to do any act in violation of the lawful duty of such official or person;

(2) being a public official or person selected to be a public official, directly or indirectly, corruptly demands, seeks, receives, accepts, or agrees to

receive or accept anything of value personally or for any other person or entity, in return for:

(A) being influenced in the performance of any official act;

(B) being influenced to commit or aid in committing, or to collude in, or allow, any fraud, or make opportunity for the commission of any fraud, on the United States; or

(C) being induced to do or omit to do any act in violation of the official duty of such official or person;

(3) directly or indirectly, corruptly gives, offers, or promises anything of value to any person, or offers or promises such person to give anything of value to any other person or entity, with intent to influence the testimony under oath or affirmation of such first-mentioned person as a witness upon a trial, hearing, or other proceeding, before any court, any committee of either House or both Houses of Congress, or any agency, commission, or officer authorized by the laws of the United States to hear evidence or take testimony, or with intent to influence such person to absent himself therefrom;

(4) directly or indirectly, corruptly demands, seeks, receives, accepts, or agrees to receive or accept anything of value personally or for any other person or entity in return for being influenced in testimony under oath or affirmation as a witness upon any such trial, hearing, or other proceeding, or in return for absenting himself therefrom; shall be fined under this title or not more than three times the monetary equivalent of the thing of value, whichever is greater, or imprisoned for not more than fifteen years, or both, and may be disqualified from holding any office of honor, trust, or profit under the United States.

(c) Whoever—

(1) otherwise than as provided by law for the proper discharge of official duty—

(A) directly or indirectly gives, offers, or promises anything of value to any public official, former public official, or person selected to be a public official, for or because of any official act performed or to be performed by such public official, former public official, or person selected to be a public official; or

(B) being a public official, former public official, or person selected to be a public official, otherwise than as provided by law for the proper discharge of official duty, directly or indirectly demands, seeks, receives, accepts, or agrees to receive or accept anything of value personally for or because of any official act performed or to be performed by such official or person;

Israeli arms dealers have not been Perle's only collaborators. Richard Perle contracted $726,000 in contingency fees with the telecommunications company Global Crossing to secure Department of Defense clearance of the sale of the company to an Asian investor, Hutchinson Whampoa:

> "It's the latest in a series of revelations of Perle's business dealings that, at the very least, make clear why he decided against taking an official position in the administration of President George W. Bush. It seems that Perle, for all his hawkishness, wants to get rich in ways that government service may not permit.
>
> Those business dealings, which include interests in companies selling advanced computer eavesdropping systems and other 'homeland security'-related systems to foreign intelligence and security agencies,

have raised ethical questions about whether he is using his unpaid position as chairman of the Pentagon's Defense Policy Board (DPB) for personal gain. While the latest disclosure about his relationship with Global Crossing also raises ethical issues, the fact that China is involved—Beijing being considered by most neo-cons the power most likely to challenge US regional dominance in Asia—makes the case even more remarkable.

According to a notice submitted by Global Crossing, Perle would be paid US$726,000 by the company, including $600,000 if the sale goes through. Whether it will remains unclear, however. Both the Defense Department and the Federal Bureau of Investigation (FBI) have raised some 'national security' problems with the deal because it would put Global Crossing's global fiber-optics network, which is used by the Pentagon itself, under Hutchison Whampoa's control." **Jim Lobe, Asia Times**[140]

Again, Perle is in violation of laws that prohibit this type of graft by government officials.

## USC 18 > PART I > CHAPTER 11 > § 208
## Acts affecting a personal financial interest

(a) Except as permitted by subsection (b) hereof, whoever, being an officer or employee of the executive branch of the United States Government, or of any independent agency of the United States, a Federal Reserve bank director, officer, or employee, or an officer or employee of the District of Columbia, including a special Government employee, participates personally and substantially as a Government officer or employee, through decision, approval, disapproval, recommendation, the rendering of advice, investigation, or otherwise, in a judicial or other proceeding, application, request for a ruling or other determination, contract, claim, controversy, charge, accusation, arrest, or other particular matter in which, to his knowledge, he, his spouse, minor child, general partner, organization in which he is serving as officer, director, trustee, general partner or employee, or any person or organization with whom he is negotiating or has any arrangement concerning prospective employment, has a financial interest—

Shall be subject to the penalties set forth in section 216 of this title.

While the aforementioned cases are not an exhaustive list of the graft, extortion, and general corruption of leading neoconservatives, they should lead investigators and prosecutors to ask a simple question. Is the ongoing espionage, wire fraud, tax fraud, and extortion merely a series of individual crimes, or the visible manifestation of a crime syndicate?

## The Larger Crime Syndicate

Neoconservatives have put together a system of ideas, activities, and contempt for national and international law. Reductionism or prosecuting individual crimes is possible, but criminally prosecuting the sum of the parts would be even more productive. Is it simple extortion from military contractors? Or the bribing of public officials like Darleen Druyan? No, it is the extortion and misapplication through illicit means of American resources, human, financial, and industrial. It is the culmination of forces in which Darlene Druyan was playing third violin in Richard Perle and Frank Gaffney's orchestra. Is it the manipulation of elections or AIPAC directing a legally separate and independent body of astroturf PACs with the input of neocon think tanks and intellectuals? No, the crime is in the unfit and compromised officials that this corrupt process brings to office. Is it the fact that mainstream media promotes and gives the last say on most military and foreign policy analysis to highly subsidized neoconservative "news sources"? No, the crime is the "dumbing down" of the debate in America, walling off legitimate lines of inquiry, and resultant wholly misinformed and misled American public. The crime is robbing Hollinger shareholders to exclusively promote ideas that have too little merit to receive an airing otherwise.

The crime is decision-making under the threat of unjustifiable intimidation and a menu of false choices. The crime is removing options from the American body politic and replacing them with a hair-trigger military "first strike" mechanism. It is a US Treasury bankrupted and mortgaged for the future by wasteful and unwarranted military spending.

The neocon network most resembles a new type of Mafia: a group of interacting individuals of power and status who fulfill particular functions in the crime syndicate. Neocons have grown more reticent to discuss their interactions as time has passed, even to the point of denying that there is much interaction or coordination.

> "In truth, the people labeled neocons (con is short for 'conservative' and neo is short for 'Jewish') travel in widely different circles and don't actually have much contact with one another." **David Brooks, 12/30/2003**

Before the invasion of Iraq and increased scrutiny of neoconservatives, key players were more candid about roles within the network:

## Neocons: America's New Mafia?

"Frank [Gaffney] keeps the network of Reagan Administration national security people together."
**Douglas Feith, 1995**

The crimes of the neocon network are not simply the reducible sum of their parts: they are the irreducible interaction of the complex elements of the system. Like the Mafia, Japanese Yakuza, Indian Thuggees, and other gangster networks, the system is a crime network that distributes illicit remuneration while synthesizing crimes. Unlike traditional crime syndicates, it is capable of murdering hundreds of thousands, if not millions, while grafting billions of dollars. Like any organized crime syndicate, neocons play different roles within their organization. Some, like Joel Mowbray and David Horowitz,[141] are media hit men, publicly assassinating the character of opponents who raise questions about neoconservative activities. Others circulate between the government and the military-industrial complex as million-dollar bagmen.

## La Cosa Nuovo – Leadership Structure and Duties

| Hierarchy | Traditional Role/Job Description in the Mafia | Current Leadership | Role/Job Description in La Cosa Nuovo |
|---|---|---|---|
| *Capo di Tutti Capi* | The "Boss of Bosses," currently Bernardo "Il Trattore" Provenzano for the Sicilian Mafia; not usually applicable to the American Mafia | Richard Perle | Broker and "close" major money deals such as Boeing, th Saudi extortion, ar the Iraq invasion |
| *Capo di Capi Re* | A title of respect given to a senior or retired member, equivalent to being a member *emeritus* | Paul Wolfowitz | Defining strategie major policy initiatives |
| *Capo Crimini* | A "Super Boss" known as a Don or "Godfather" of a crime family | Norman Podheretz, Irving Kristol, Douglas Feith | Softer tone and intellectual sheen, coordination and implementation |
| *Capo Bastone* | Known as the "Underboss," second in command to the *Capo Crimini* | William Kristol | Propagation of ideological discipline, spreadi the word |
| *Consigliere* | An advisor | David Brooks | Public image, soft messages, alignme |
| *Contabile* | A financial advisor | Frank Gaffney, Jack Abramoff | Ongoing fundraisi and PR service as military deal brok |

## Neocons: America's New Mafia?

| Hierarchy | Traditional Role/Job Description in the Mafia | Current Leadership | Role/Job Description in La Cosa Nuovo |
|---|---|---|---|
| *Caporegime* or *Capodecina* | A lieutenant who commands a "crew" of around ten *Sgarrista* or "soldiers" | Lawrence Franklin | Espionage, end runs around institutional barriers, fall guy |
| *Sgarrista* or *Soldati* | "Made" members of the Mafia who serve primarily as foot soldiers | Michael Ledeen | Dirty work, Iran Contra-Italian forgeries, espionage |
| *Picciotto* | A low-ranking member who serves as an "enforcer" | Jonah Goldberg, Joel Mowbray, David Horowitz | "Enforcement" through smear, defamation in the news media |
| *Giovane D'Onore* | An associate member, usually not of Italian or Sicilian ancestry | George Will | Ideological backing, implementation, appearance of diversity |

As with the Italian Mafia in the US, there is a strong group orientation to a foreign "homeland," but in this case it is a highly idealized concept of Israel rather than Sicily. The mix of neocon business, media savvy, and talking points circulates through the upper reaches of American society and the foreign policy establishment, from Georgetown University to "Think Tank Row" on Massachusetts Avenue. Their high profile provides the appearance of legitimacy and overshadows the dark underbelly of a much broader racket.

## *Conclusions*

Neocon dogma is deadly. After their proactive substitution of slogans and noble lies for honest research and contemplation, America has become less able to make the sound decisions that our system of government would otherwise have produced.

The influence of neocon thinking and policy on the US can be directly linked to ongoing military contract fraud, propaganda and wire fraud, espionage, graft, tax evasion, and other crimes against the US.

Although it is the currently preferred tool for challenging robust crime syndicates, the Racketeer-Influenced Corrupt Organization (RICO) statute is ill-configured to prosecute the neocon network as it truly is: a sophisticated crime syndicate. It has been tried (see Hollinger Shareholders vs. Richard Perle) and failed.

Fortunately, criminal statutes that are already on the books can provide a remedy. With prosecutorial will, buttressed by the growing chorus of demands from the American people, the damage of deadly neocon dogma can be nullified. This dogma's influence on the United States can be rolled back so that common sense, historical evidence, reason, and uncorrupted thinking may again navigate the ship of state.

America's way forward may depend on the US Department of Justice's capacity to look back into the history of unpunished neoconservative lawbreaking.

# Appendix A: PNAC Letter to Bill Clinton

January 26, 1998

The Honorable William J. Clinton
President of the United States
Washington, DC

Dear Mr. President:

We are writing you because we are convinced that current American policy toward Iraq is not succeeding, and that we may soon face a threat in the Middle East more serious than any we have known since the end of the Cold War. In your upcoming State of the Union Address, you have an opportunity to chart a clear and determined course for meeting this threat. We urge you to seize that opportunity, and to enunciate a new strategy that would secure the interests of the U.S. and our friends and allies around the world. That strategy should aim, above all, at the removal of Saddam Hussein's regime from power. We stand ready to offer our full support in this difficult but necessary endeavor.

The policy of "containment" of Saddam Hussein has been steadily eroding over the past several months. As recent events have demonstrated, we can no longer depend on our partners in the Gulf War coalition to continue to uphold the sanctions or to punish Saddam when he blocks or evades UN inspections. Our ability to ensure that Saddam Hussein is not producing weapons of mass destruction, therefore, has substantially diminished. Even if full inspections were eventually to resume, which now seems highly unlikely, experience has shown that it is difficult if not impossible to monitor Iraq's chemical and biological weapons production. The lengthy period during which the inspectors will have been unable to enter many Iraqi facilities has made it even less likely that they will be able to uncover all of Saddam's secrets. As a result, in the not-too-distant future we will be unable to determine with any reasonable level of confidence whether Iraq does or does not possess such weapons.

Such uncertainty will, by itself, have a seriously destabilizing effect on the entire Middle East. It hardly needs to be added that if Saddam does acquire the capability to deliver weapons of mass destruction, as he is almost certain to do if we continue along the present course, the safety of American troops in the region, of our friends and allies like Israel and the moderate Arab states, and a significant portion of the world's supply of oil will all be put at hazard. As you have rightly declared, Mr. President, the security of the world in the first part of the 21st century will be determined largely by how we handle this threat.

Given the magnitude of the threat, the current policy, which depends for its success upon the steadfastness of our coalition partners and upon the cooperation of Saddam Hussein, is dangerously inadequate. The only acceptable strategy is one that eliminates the possibility that Iraq will be able to use or threaten to use weapons of mass destruction. In the near term, this means a willingness to undertake military action as diplomacy is clearly failing. In the long term, it means removing Saddam Hussein and his regime from power. That now needs to become the aim of American foreign policy.

We urge you to articulate this aim, and to turn your Administration's attention to implementing a strategy for removing Saddam's regime from power. This will require a full complement of diplomatic, political and military efforts. Although we are fully aware of the dangers and difficulties in implementing this policy, we believe the dangers of failing to do so are far greater. We believe the U.S. has the authority under existing UN resolutions to take the necessary steps, including military steps, to protect our vital interests in the

Gulf. In any case, American policy cannot continue to be crippled by a misguided insistence on unanimity in the UN Security Council.

We urge you to act decisively. If you act now to end the threat of weapons of mass destruction against the U.S. or its allies, you will be acting in the most fundamental national security interests of the country. If we accept a course of weakness and drift, we put our interests and our future at risk.

Sincerely,

Elliott Abrams    Richard L. Armitage    William J. Bennett

Jeffrey Bergner    John Bolton    Paula Dobriansky

Francis Fukuyama    Robert Kagan    Zalmay Khalilzad

William Kristol    Richard Perle    Peter W. Rodman

Donald Rumsfeld    William Schneider, Jr.    Vin Weber

Paul Wolfowitz    R. James Woolsey    Robert B. Zoellick

# Appendix B: Arab-Israeli Crisis and War, 1967

Declassified and Released by the Office of the Historian in January 12 of 2004

We include the entire corpus of cables, international memos and deliberation since, to date, most historians covering the 1967 Six Day War have not adequately addressed the US-Egyptian efforts to wind down the conflict, nor have the formerly classified communications and documents appeared widely in print.

**Documents 129-148**

### 129. Telegram From the Embassy in Portugal to the Department of State/1/

Lisbon, June 2, 1967, 1030Z.

/1/Source: National Archives and Records Administration, RG 59, Central Files 1967-69, POL ARAB-ISR. Top Secret; Immediate; Nodis. Received at 8:29 a.m. Walt Rostow sent a copy to the President at 12:40 p.m. with a memorandum stating, "It is urgent that we decide whether we should inform the Israelis of this visit. **My guess is their intelligence will pick it up.** We would be wise to have Sec. Rusk tell Harman." He also added, "In the light of this picture of Nasser's mind, we must work out most carefully the scenario for talks with Mohieddin." (Johnson Library, National Security File, Country File, Middle East Crisis, Anderson Cables)

**1517. Eyes Only for President and SecState from Robert Anderson.**

## Deadly Dogma:
## How Neoconservatives Broke the Law to Deceive America

1. There follows a summary of my talk with President Nasser. Unless otherwise indicated, I will be trying to express his point of view to me.

2. After exchange of pleasantries, Nasser said he became worried and afraid of Israeli attack because of speeches and his own intelligence of mobilization by Israel and the intelligence shared with Syrian Govt. As an example, he stated that 13 brigades were mobilized near Syria.

3. Nasser explained that he did not want repetition of 1956 affair when he was reluctant to believe that an attack had begun and was slow in moving troops to Sinai only to be caught between the Israelis in the north and the British at Port Said. He said he felt he had no choice but to mobilize and send troops to Sinai, which he did, and request the removal of UN forces. While he did not say so, I believe he was surprised at the rapidity of the removal of UN troops because he said they were only a token force and would have created no real obstacle.

4. He was asked specifically if he intended to begin any conflict and he said to please explain to my govt that he would not begin any fight but would wait until the Israelis had moved. This was qualified by saying that he did not know what the Syrians would do and had worried all day (Wednesday)/2/ for fear the Syrians might start something out of anger because of the pact which he had made with Hussein. He also stated, that, contrary to most public opinion, he did not have control over the radical elements of refugee organizations who were interested only in starting a conflict because they had no real responsibility for the conduct of military affairs. He was asked if this conflict occurred, for example, if Syria should attack against his desires, whether he would respond and he answered affirmatively, saying that any conflict begun, whether in Jordan or Syria, would necessarily bring response from him.

/2/May 31.

5. It was pointed out that if Israel felt she was virtually alone she might be motivated to strike first in order to secure a strategic advantage and that so long as she felt she had friends she might be restrained. Nasser replied that this was a risk which he would have to accept and that he thought first Israeli target and main thrust of Israeli offensive would be against Egypt and Cairo. He said that elaborate plans had been made for instant retaliation, and that he was confident of the outcome of a conflict between Arabs and Israelis.

6. Nasser said that Hussein requested a meeting with him and that he agreed on the basis that it would be secret unless an agreement was reached between them. Nasser then consulted with the govts of

Morocco, Algeria, Iraq and Syria. All of these agreed that some agreement with Hussein was desirable except Syria who was opposed to any agreement with Jordan. He was asked if he had consulted directly or indirectly [with] the Saudi Arabs and he replied that he had no contact, direct or indirect, with the Saudi Arabs or Faisal. However, Nasser felt that Faisal was in a difficult position and could not avoid participation if fighting began.

7. With reference to Gulf of Aqaba, Nasser stated that for eight years after 1948 the Straits had been closed to Israeli shipping and was open only by the illegal act of Israel, France and England, and he proposed merely to return to the status of 1956 which had been at least tolerated by all the nations for eight years. He explained that even we had deplored and opposed the act of the Israelis, British and French which changed the status quo in 1956. He stated that the Straits of Tiran were navigable only in a width of three miles which was clearly territorial waters and that he intended to maintain this position. He was asked specifically what commerce he would allow through the Straits under his concept and he replied by saying that the exclusions would be 1) Israeli ships, 2) oil or any refined products, and 3) arms for Israel. Here he stated that all countries claimed territorial waters to a greater distance offshore than he was asserting and further that he was at war with Israel and had been since 1948 with nothing existing between them except an armistice, and that under these circumstances he was entitled to assert jurisdiction.

8. He was asked if he would consider referring this matter of the Straits to either the United Nations or the World Court, in view of the fact that four countries had borders on the Gulf. He replied that he would not submit the question to the UN because the Israelis normally treated resolutions of the UN not favorable to them as "pieces of paper." He said that he did not have sufficient knowledge of the World Court to answer specifically about referring the matter to the World Court for decision but would consult his legal advisers. This was qualified by saying that he did not want to undertake any course of action that would take "years" to decide.

9. He also stated that even if he agreed on some other course of action, any other course of action would be strongly opposed by all Arab countries who were now his allies. On this point he seemed on the one hand adamant about the position he had taken in the Straits and yet he did not rule out completely possibility of a World Court review if it could be done speedily. For the time being I think he will remain firm.

10. He was asked if he was not prepared to accept Israel as a matter of fact, even though he might have emotional and legal feelings

concerning the establishment of the country in Palestine. Nasser replied by saying that he did not believe stable and lasting peace could be achieved without disposing of the refugee problem. He was asked if this could be done by compensation as well as some limited return of refugees. He replied that he thought practically all refugees would return if permitted and that even if compensation were paid they would not be satisfied but would continue to agitate for return to Palestine. He went into long discourse on Arab mentality as it affects their feelings toward the place where they were born and reared.

11. Nasser stated that he had been prepared to sign an agreement with the Monetary Fund but had just received a letter saying that the Fund wished to review their relationships with Egypt further. He then stated he was glad he had not signed the agreement with the Fund because they were unreasonable and left him no flexibility. He emphasized that he did not want to be subject to economic pressure. It was explained to him that neither the Fund nor local American banks were in fact exerting pressure when they did not comply with national requests since they were all governed by strict rules that limited their own flexibility in making loans to countries that did not comply with all regulations.

12. Nasser expressed keen desire to have friendship of American people and American Govt explaining that under no circumstances was he a Communist. On other hand, he felt that US policy was motivated largely by the large Jewish vote in US and that American Govt would be reluctant to oppose this voting strength. He then called attention to the fact that Eisenhower had taken a strong position in 1956 against Israeli invasion and this had not hurt him politically.

13. He seemed anxious to have Zakaria Mohieddin explain his position directly to US Govt and said he hoped we would take the long view because the Arab countries stretched from Morocco on the west to Pakistan on the east and that now he even had the support of Pakistan and India. He did not see how a minority in the US could influence US policy to oppose what such a vast region and such large numbers of people believed proper. It was explained to him that the US Govt was not motivated by political considerations but was concerned essentially in maintaining peace and the integrity of countries.

14. At this time Nasser said that if the policy was for Arabs and Israelis to live together harmoniously and Israel should allow a million refugees to come back to Palestine, which would solve the refugee problem and still the Israelis would have two million of their own citizens in the same country, this, he said, would be true "living together."

15. He made it clear that he felt US was taking the lead in peace efforts but that these efforts were oriented toward Israel and not toward the Arab point of view. He kept reassuring me that he was not going to start a war but that he was not responsible for all groups and that he would intervene in any actual conflict begun. He stated that under present circumstances Jordanian troops, insofar as the Israeli problem was concerned, were under UAR command. This of course is applicable to other troops such as Iraqis and Algerians who were reporting for duty.

16. This I think summarizes the basic points of our conversation on which I will elaborate further on my return.

17. For your general information I spent three days in Beirut before going to Cairo. During this visit I saw Saudi Arabs, Kuwaitis and Iraqis, as well as Lebanese. They are people who are generally moderate and have a tendency to oppose Nasser. At this time they were all applauding Nasser's action, insisting on the closing of the Gulf of Aqaba and taking a position that the US was supporting a minority for political purposes. I am impressed more because of the quality of the people who made these assertions than the fact that they were made. Under the circumstances it would seem desirable that whatever international arrangements are thought proper it would be helpful if the initiative could be taken by some country other than US and that US be in a position of support of international efforts to secure peace rather than leadership which seems to be construed as favoring Israeli cause.

17. [sic] During our conversation Nasser was relaxed, in sport clothes, and seemed confident both of his intelligence and of his military capability. We had no discussion re Soviets except his assertion that he was not and would not be Communist. I believe he would regard any effort to open the Straits of Tiran as hostile and any act of aggression, whether originating from Israel or resulting from actions in Syria by the terrorist groups, would bring response. He stated that his target system was prepared and that this time he would be ready.

18. I am proceeding to send message to Cairo through US Embassy to Nasser which will result in Zakaria Mohieddin arriving in New York presumably Sunday or early in week. I will return to New York Saturday/3/ afternoon and will be available to come to Washington Sunday or thereafter. I can be reached through Embassy here today and tomorrow morning, if desired.

/3/June 3.

19. Upon rereading this text I want to make clear as I understand it UAR has military command over its own troops, the Jordanian troops as related to any Israeli problem, the troops committed by Iraq, Algeria or any country sending troops, but does not include command over Syrian troops. It is because of this latter situation which I think bothers Nasser as to whether or not the Syrians might undertake unilateral action designed to force a confrontation. It was because of his concern on this subject that he was asked if he would intervene even if the Syrians acted against UAR desires and the reply was affirmative.

Wellman

### 130. Memorandum of Conversation/1/

Washington, June 2, 1967, 11:30 a.m.-1:15 p.m.

/1/Source: National Archives and Records Administration, RG 59, Central Files 1967-69, POL 27 ARAB-ISR. Secret. Drafted by Assistant Secretary of State for European Affairs Leddy and approved by the White House and S on June 14. The memorandum is part I of IV. The meeting took place in the Cabinet Room of the White House. At the same time (11:35 a.m. to 1:30 p.m.), President Johnson and Prime Minister Wilson met privately in the Oval Office. (Johnson Library, President's Daily Diary) No record of their meeting has been found.

SUBJECT

Middle East

PARTICIPANTS

*Americans present*
Secretary of State
Secretary of the Treasury (part time)
Secretary of Defense
Ambassador Bruce
Mr. Walt Rostow (part time)
EUR--Mr. John M. Leddy
Mr. Francis Bator (part time)
S/CPR--Mr. James W. Symington

*British present:*
Sir Burke Trend, Secretary of the Cabinet
Sir Patrick Dean, Ambassador

Admiral Sir Nigel Henderson, Head, British Defense Staff
Sir Solly Zuckerman, Chief Scientific Advisor
T. T. Brenchley, Assistant Secretary Foreign Office
Donald Murray, Head, South East Asian Department, Foreign Office
A. N. Halls, Principal Private Secretary to Prime Minister
A. M. Palliser, Private Secretary to Prime Minister
T. D. Floyd-Huges, Press Secretary to Prime Minister

This conversation ranged over various aspects of the Arab-Israeli confrontation in the Middle East and lasted about an hour and a half. The following brings together the main substantive points brought out in the discussion.

*Security Council Action*

There are now two resolutions on this subject in the Security Council: the American resolution and the Egyptian resolution. Possibly two more resolutions will be submitted, including one from India. The Secretary felt that there was virtually no chance for any resolution to be agreed upon and that the inability of the Council to act would probably become clear next Tuesday/2/ or Wednesday. However, even if the Council was unable to adopt a resolution, it was important to have the Council remain seized of the problem. It was just possible that as events develop certain prestige elements can be thrown into the Council machinery as happened in the case of the Cuban missile crisis.

/2/June 6.

*Limits on Israeli Restraint*

The Secretary observed that we have a breathing spell for the moment, but unless there is some change in Nasser's intentions regarding the Straits of Tiran this will not last long and **it will be impossible to hold the Israelis.** We had a great deal of difficulty with them last Sunday/3/ when the decision in the Israeli Cabinet to hold back for the time being was very close (9 to 9). The new Cabinet was meeting again this coming Sunday or Monday and we may face a crisis. **The appointment of Moshe Dayan as Defense Minister was hardly favorable to restraint.** Secretary McNamara thought that the one thing which might deter the Israelis would be their fear that the Soviets might enter a war on the side of the Arabs.

/3/May 28.

*Israeli/Arab Military Capabilities*

Secretary McNamara said that the Israelis feel that they could start hostilities now or a week from now and prevail. They believe their capabilities are perishable as time goes on, but Secretary McNamara thought they could delay from 2-4 weeks and still accomplish their military objective. They would try to destroy the Egyptian airforce first and thus gain ability for a tank strike to take Sinai and the Straits.

**Secretary McNamara said the Israelis think they can win in 3-4 days; but he thinks it would be longer--7 to 10 days.**

Secretary McNamara said that the Israelis felt that they could not keep up their mobilization for more than a week or two. He believed that they could sustain it for a longer time economically (it is costing them about $1 million a day); but the real problem is political and because of this they probably would have to act within two weeks. The economic strain of mobilization was much greater on the Israelis in their tight manpower situation than on the Arabs with their large unemployment.

Sir Burke Trend, in response to a question from Secretary McNamara, said that the UK military analysis of the Israeli capabilities was close to that of the US but perhaps a bit more conservative and rested on the assumption that the Israelis would not let things go too long. Both sides agreed that an Israeli military success would take more than a few days and possibly a week plus. Certainly it would take longer than it took in 1956 and it would be bloodier.

Sir Burke Trend inquired what effect an Arab-Israeli war would have on Egypt's ability to maintain its forces in Yemen. Secretary McNamara said he did not have a firm opinion. His best guess is that they could contain the military--it was a very small force--but that it would be politically difficult for Nasser to do so at the moment when he is faced with an all-out Israeli attack.

The Secretary thought that the worst problem that would face the US would be if the Israelis were defeated and were about to be driven into the sea. Secretary McNamara doubted that the Israelis would lose; and that we would have a real problem if the Soviets came in to save Egypt.

Sir Burke Trend thought that Nasser may have his eye on the next step--beyond the Straits problem. The Secretary thought that Nasser was riding a tiger. He had been preaching Jihad or Holy War. If it doesn't occur, or if the Straits don't remain closed, he may find it impossible to restrain popular passions.

*Situation in the Straits*

The Secretary said that although there had earlier been some confusion on the point it was now clear that the Egyptian blockade covered oil--in other words it is the Battle Act list plus oil. It was not yet clear however what the Egyptians would do if a non-Israeli flagship carrying oil for Eilat should attempt passage.

The Secretary observed that there were two passages into the Gulf of Aqaba other than the Straits of Tiran; one of these--the Enterprise Passage--appeared to be navigable and was some four miles from the Egyptian coast. The navigability of the third passage was in some doubt. Both of these possibilities should be looked into. Secretary McNamara said it was highly unlikely that these have been mined.

It was brought out in the discussion that no ship so far had transited to Eilat; all have gone into Aqaba in Jordan.

The Secretary observed that Israeli access to Eilat is not really vital in an economic sense. The question is rather political. The Israelis consider that they have had a firm international commitment for guaranteed access since 1957 and the legitimacy of their territorial position in Eilat is not really in doubt.

*The Soviet Attitude*

Both sides felt that the Soviets probably had not been informed by Nasser of his intended action regarding the Straits of Tiran. In their public statements the Soviets have carefully skirted the question of the Straits, simply supporting the Egyptian claim to territorial waters which is beside the point. We have nothing back ourselves from the Soviets on the Straits question.

The Secretary thought that if the Israelis attack and are winning that the Soviets would do "something;" they would "help;" but we do not really know what kind of help this would be. He observed that apparently both the Arabs and the Soviets think the US is capable of commanding Israel.

*Anderson Report*

171

## Deadly Dogma:
## How Neoconservatives Broke the Law to Deceive America

The Secretary paraphrased a cable which had just been received reporting on Robert Anderson's conversation with Nasser./4/ (The Secretary made it clear that Anderson was in Egypt in an entirely private capacity.) The Secretary wondered about the reference in Anderson's report to Nasser's apparent willingness to envisage World Court consideration provided that the Court would act in a hurry. This made no sense unless Nasser anticipated maintaining freedom of passage pending the Court's decision.

*Economic and Financial Aspects*

/4/See Document 129.

Sir Burke Trend wondered what economic pressures might be brought to bear against the Arabs. Secretary Fowler pointed out that more economic and financial pressure could be exercised from the other side than from ours--cutting off of oil exports, expropriation, monetary measures damaging to sterling, etc. The Egyptians can depend on the Soviets for wheat and on the Kuwaitis for money. He observed that the recent failure of the IMF to extend a $30 million loan to the UAR was not really so disadvantageous to the Egyptians since the main purpose of the credit was to enable them to make good on their default to private banks and reestablish their credit position.

The Secretary thought that with respect to the Israelis other countries could help. He would not be surprised if the Israelis didn't get as much as $100 million from the American Jewish community.

Commenting on the British financial situation, Secretary Fowler felt that outstanding swaps, including those with the Continent, provided a healthy cushion. It would be undesirable to try to improve the situation in advance of hostilities since it would cause speculation. It was agreed on both sides that for the time being at least the market was in fairly good shape.

The Secretary pointed out that if the Arabs should do anything to cut off the flow of oil Europe would face a serious shortfall even with maximum supplies from the Western Hemisphere.

*Proposed Maritime Declaration*

Responding to Sir Burke Trend, Secretary McNamara said that the circular instruction on the Maritime Declaration/5/ had just gone out last night and it was too early to have had a response. Mr. Leddy expressed the opinion that it would not be too bad a result if we could get as many as twelve countries lined up behind us. No doubt there would be questions as to whether this Declaration implied the use of force. When it was made clear that it did not it would make things somewhat easier. Later in the day the Secretary said perhaps we could get as many as 20 or 30.

/5/Document 111.

Sir Burke Trend suggested that perhaps after the Maritime Declaration had been issued the powers supporting the Declaration might propose a specific convention dealing with the Strait of Tiran and the Gulf of Aqaba. The Secretary thought that perhaps the Arabs might come to a conference on this subject if called by the Secretary General of the UN. However, he recalled that the Aqaba clause in the Convention in 1958 had been adopted 31-30 with 10 abstentions. The Arabs would no doubt use the "belligerent" argument and assert that the 1956 resolution had been imposed by aggression. He observed that the Montreux Convention on the Bosporus/6/ provided a precedent for the Trend proposal.

/6/The Montreux Convention, signed June 20, 1936, by Britain, Bulgaria, France, Japan, Rumania, the Soviet Union, and Turkey; for text, see *League of Nations Treaty Series,* Vol. CLXXIII, p. 213.

The Declaration speaks of "asserting rights" to innocent passage in the Straits. Sir Burke Trend inquired what was meant by asserting rights other than through the use of force. The Secretary replied that this could cover various actions such as public statements, appeals to the World Court, proposed UN resolutions, economic reprisals, etc. He suggested that at some point it might be useful to introduce the Declaration into the UN machinery in order to keep the talk going. For example, the Danish Chairman of the Security Council might possibly use this in talking with the Arabs.

*Possible Naval Task Force*

Secretaries Rusk and McNamara made it very clear that any participation by the US in the use of force would have to be supported by Congressional action. We have consulted intensively with the Congressional leaders in the last ten days. It is clear that there is a passionate aversion on the Hill to any unilateral action by the US. We would have to have UN action or at least broad multilateral participation. If we were to ask for Congressional support at this moment we could not get it. We will first have to continue our efforts in the UN and achieve multilateral support for the Maritime Declaration.

## Deadly Dogma:
## How Neoconservatives Broke the Law to Deceive America

Secretary McNamara recalled that Secretary Dulles in 1956-57 had made it very clear that Congressional action would be required for the use of force in the Middle East.

In a further discussion of this point it was agreed on both sides that there would be no US-UK joint planning in the military field at this stage. The danger of leaks was too great. The British side indicated that it, too, was hesitant to move too fast in the military area.

### Possible Appointment of Mediator

There was some discussion of the possible naming of a mediator. Perhaps someone like Gus Lindt, Swiss Ambassador to Moscow.

Sir Burke Trend inquired what a mediator might conceivably do in terms of speculation. The Secretary replied that one thing he might do would be to try to persuade each side of the consequence of a war and from a realization of this perhaps build toward a way out. He observed that this was the way the Berlin crisis had been handled.

### Position of Prime Minister Pearson

Secretary McNamara asked about Pearson's position on the use of force. Sir Burke Trend said that Pearson was not yet ready to answer.

The Secretary inquired whether Pearson might not play a mediating role as he had in the past. The British side said he felt that he would be regarded by the Arabs as being too biased.

### U Thant

Both sides agreed that SYG U Thant had acted precipitately in removing the UNEF. The Secretary pointed out that he had gone beyond what Nasser requested and had moved faster than Nasser expected. Moreover, the Secretary understood that during U Thant's trip to Cairo he had proposed to the Egyptians a strategic embargo including oil but that the Israelis had turned this down. The question was why did U Thant feel that he had the right to make an offer of this kind?

### Egypt's Use of Gas in Yemen

The British asked why the US has not made public the Egyptian use of gas in Yemen. The Secretary replied that this information would have greater impact internationally if it came from the Red Cross rather than from the US. Mr. Rostow said that we had just released a report to the four governments concerned and planned to publish text he thought about June 5 or 6. (Reference to the report appeared in *The New York Times* on June 3.)

*Future Joint Planning*

Ambassador Dean raised the question of further planning. He said that there were four separate areas: political; military; oil; and finance. He thought that we should keep these four areas under some kind of overall control and also to give consideration to making them multilateral at some stage.

It was again pointed out by Secretaries Rusk and McNamara that it was too early for military planning (for example, it would have been disastrous if we had been caught in military planning last week) and that we will just have to see how things develop. Secretary Fowler emphasized the importance of immediate planning in both the financial and oil fields. We would be derelict if we did not plan for these.

The following appeared to be generally agreed:

1. There would be a small group on overall matters on the US side to keep in touch with a similar group on the UK side.

2. Military planning was out for the time being.

3. The British are ready to come to Washington to talk about oil next week.

4. Monetary and financial discussions should be developed between the US and the UK through established official channels including the two Treasuries, the Bank of England and the New York Fed. There should be no approaches to the private sector at this stage because of the dangers of speculation.

**131. Memorandum From the President's Special Assistant (Rostow) to President Johnson/1/**

# Deadly Dogma:
## How Neoconservatives Broke the Law to Deceive America

Washington, June 2, 1967, 12:45 p.m.

/1/Source: Johnson Library, National Security File, Country File, Middle East Crisis, Vol. III. Secret; Eyes Only. A handwritten "L" on the memorandum indicates the President saw it. Saunders sent a copy to John Walsh with a memorandum of December 10, 1968, commenting that the memorandum was the clearest statement "on whether we had a 'commitment' from Eshkol to wait two weeks." He added, however, "but even there there's a possibility of our overreading. I was there and sat through Walt's dictation of the memo and believed at the time it reflected accurately what Eppie said. But by that time, even Eppie may have been overtaken by thinking in Jerusalem." Saunders indicated that Walsh should particularly note Evron's reply to Rostow's first question in paragraph 6. (National Archives and Records Administration, RG 59, Central Files 1967-69, POL ISR-US)

Mr. President:

Evron came in today at 11:00 a.m. with the following extremely important statement. It is not (repeat not) a communication from the Government of Israel. Moreover, he underlined several times the need for it to be held within our government in the narrowest possible circle.

Nevertheless, Evron does not talk irresponsibly.

Here is his statement.

1. Time is working rapidly against Israel.

Nasser's forces are being built up and digging in. The Arab military forces are being unified and consolidated. The economic costs for Israel are rising. The political and psychological pressures for a prompt solution are increasing.

2. They took our advice to wait as a cold, responsible calculus. Nevertheless, it is now clear that the military cost to them of a war with Egypt is rising every day.

3. He then asked what our reaction would be to the following scenario:

The probe at the Gulf of Aqaba would not be made under the protection of an international armada. It would be made by an Israeli ship. The first shot would be fired by the UAR. Acting on the principle asserted by Golda Meir in the attached UN statement of 1 March 1957/2/ (to which Lodge assented),/3/ Israel would attack the installations at Sharm al-Sheikh covering the straits of Aqaba. The next move would be Nasser's. The Israelis believe he would attack Israel on a wide front and probably other Arab nations would join in the attack.

/2/Reference is to a copy of the second document that Harman gave to Eugene Rostow on May 26; see footnote 3, Document 69. It quotes paragraph 13 of Foreign Minister Golda Meir's speech of March 1, 1957, before the UN General Assembly, which reads in part: "Interference, by armed force, with ships of Israel flag exercising free and innocent passage in the Gulf of Aqaba and through the Straits of Tiran, will be regarded by Israel as an attack entitling it to exercise its inherent right of self-defence under Article 51 of the United Nations Charter and to take all such measures as are necessary to ensure the free and innocent passage of its ships in the Gulf and in the Straits."

/3/The attachment also quotes Lodge's statement before the UN General Assembly on March 1, 1957, taking note of the declarations in Meir's statement and indicating that its expectations were "not unreasonable."

4. His questions then were:

--Would the United States stand by its political commitment in 1957 that Israel under these circumstances was asserting a legitimate right of self-defense?

--Would the United States stand off any Soviet intervention in that kind of war?

5. I immediately replied that this was not a question to which I could give a responsible answer. I said that the scenario he outlined was not the one raised by Foreign Minister Eban with the President; but, obviously, it was an alternative which might be considered. I said I would report it to the President.

6. I then asked some questions on a wholly personal basis:

First: How much time did they think they had?

He replied that they had made a commitment to hold steady for about two weeks. He would measure that from the Cabinet meeting last Sunday. Therefore, he was talking about things that might happen in the week after next; that is, the week beginning Sunday, June 11--although he indicated that there was nothing ironclad about the time period being exactly two weeks.

Second, I asked him what about the stories of the Israelis buying and organizing ships to run the blockade on a national basis?

He said they were taking action of this kind; but they would not move to run the blockade without there being a clear political decision in Israel, of which we would be made aware.

7. Two other points emerged in the final stage of our conversation. First, he appeared to suggest that it might be better for us in our relations with both the Arab world and the Soviet Union if we were not the ones to force the issue. He also referred to intelligence which we share that Nasser's response to a U.S.-escorted probe would be not to fire. Therefore, the issue of Israeli access to the Gulf of Aqaba might be left hanging indecisively.

8. Second--and fundamental to his whole presentation--was the question: Do we still stand by Lodge's assent (and Foster Dulles') to Golda Meir's statement in General Assembly? The track discussed between Eban and the President--on which we have hitherto been moving--is consistent with the commitments made in 1957 that we would ourselves assert the right of innocent passage; that we would assert that right on behalf of others; but that we would have to engage through our constitutional processes if we were to use force to assert that right with force on behalf of others. What is involved in the track he is suggesting is reaffirmation of the other branch of our 1957 commitment incorporated in the Golda Meir statement and Lodge's assent.

WWR comment: Although it cannot be emphasized too strongly that Evron was not making a formal communication from his Government, I believe we should most urgently consider the track he suggests. It has always been an alternative. It has its attractions, as one measures up the consequences for our relations with the Arab world and the Soviet Union, as compared to that which was agreed with Eban. It also carries the risk of a terrible blood bath. There is also the possibility of a combined scenario--in which the Israelis assume responsibility for responding to attack on their flag ship, but against the background of a naval force standing by to shepherd through other flagships. But this--like the Eban scenario--would require a prior Congressional Resolution.

# Appendix B: Arab-Israeli Crisis and War, 1967

Walt

## 132. Memorandum of Conversation/1/

Washington, June 2, 1967, 3:47-4:45 p.m.

/1/Source: National Archives and Records Administration, RG 59, Central Files 1967-69, POL ISR-US. Top Secret; Nodis. Drafted by Davies. The time is from Rusk's Appointment Book. (Johnson Library)

SUBJECT
Near East Crisis

PARTICIPANTS

H. E. Avraham Harman, Ambassador of Israel
Mr. Ephraim Evron, Minister of Israel

The Secretary
M--Mr. Eugene V. Rostow
NEA--Rodger P. Davies

Ambassador Harman, departing for consultation in Israel within a few hours, had asked to see the Secretary to learn what he could tell his government concerning U.S. assurances of support. The Secretary responded that at this juncture nothing could be added to what the President had already communicated to Prime Minister Eshkol.

In answer to Ambassador Harman's question on the Maritime Declaration, the Secretary said we hoped to get at least 14 adherents. Both the Dutch and the Belgians seemed to be aboard and, since Costa Rica supported the principle in 1957, we hoped to get support from this country and other Latin American states. The reaction in Bonn had been encouraging, but it might be well if Israel could work on the French and Canadians who seemed to be lagging.

Ambassador Harman said reports of Portuguese support for the Declaration were embarrassing since the Africans would be extremely sensitive to anything supported by Portugal. The important thing to Israel is the timetable. We should assure the closing off of Security Council action soon; the longer it runs on, the more difficulties there will be. Already the "breathing spell" was giving rise to rumors and reports of "deals".

## Deadly Dogma:
## *How Neoconservatives Broke the Law to Deceive America*

The Secretary said that apparently there had been a complete misrepresentation of the U.S. Government's position on the Declaration stemming from briefings that had been given in the Congress. It might ease matters if the Declaration could be made public, but we could not move in this direction until other governments had a chance to discuss it. We hope it can be released when it is clear that the Security Council can do nothing on the problem.

In answer to the Ambassador's question, the Secretary said that the key issue was return to the status quo ante on use of the Gulf of Aqaba. Nasser, however, was firm on his present stand. Whether he can be moved is anybody's question. The Secretary indicated that the Maritime Declaration might provide a "handle" for the Secretary General to take further action and indicated that we have not had anything back from the Soviets on their attitude toward the question of the Strait.

The Ambassador asked whether he could faithfully report that the USG position is that there must be a return to the status quo ante, that there would be no "deal".

The Secretary said this was what we were seeking to bring about. In the Security Council it is apparent that the Soviets would veto anything calling for the parties to forego belligerency. We believe we have eight votes in support of our draft resolution and are somewhat hopeful that we may be able to line up nine.

The Secretary said that in his talks with Iraqi Foreign Minister Pachachi/2/ he did not find any "give" in the Arab position on the Gulf. Mr. Rostow said that he detected a little more flexibility in the course of his talks, although whether Pachachi had, in fact, any authority to negotiate was questionable.

/2/Rusk and Eugene Rostow met separately with Iraqi Foreign Minister Pachachi on June 1. Telegram 206672 to Baghdad, June 2, which summarized their conversations, is printed in *Foreign Relations*, 1964-1968, vol. XXI, Document 193. After meeting with Rusk and Rostow, Pachachi met with the President. No record of that conversation has been found.

The Ambassador repeated that the timetable on the Naval Task Force and next steps was of supreme importance to Israel.

The Secretary said we are going ahead on all contingencies, looking at all factors. Joint consultations would be started shortly. At present we have not developed a multilateral context, and from the Congressional angle this was of great importance. We believe the Dutch would join with us but are not sure now of the Canadians. It is important that we be joined by a half dozen or so before we can move ahead on timing. There have been no final decisions. On these, the President and the Prime Minister must be in touch.

The Ambassador said he would come to the crux of Israel's concern. The military situation is deteriorating rapidly.

Hussein's accord with Nasser, Arab military coordination, the dispatch of Iraqi troops to the UAR and Jordan, the move of Saudi troops to the Aqaba Gulf area, the big build-up of Syrian forces, the caving in of Lebanon with respect to Palestine Liberation Army (PLA) activities, and the stationing of PLA units on all frontiers are causing heightened concern in Israel. The time has come for effective resistance to Nasser. Nasser's declaration that the situation had been returned to that of 1956 was now followed by threats that it would be returned to that of 1948. Israel has mobilized 100,000 reservists in addition to its regular forces. In these circumstances Israel must know the modalities of the U.S. commitment. In addition to the direct threat to Israel of the coalescence of the Arabs around Nasser, there were ripples which must certainly concern the West, not only in connection with its position vis-a-vis the Soviets but also with the implications for Turkey and Iran. If there is a rapid show of strength in Tiran, this could affect the entire situation. Everyday the situation was allowed to continue however heightened pressures and danger. The question he would be asked in Jerusalem was: What is the attitude of the U.S. toward the question of the Strait and toward the general situation? What action would the U.S. take if hostilities began in either connection?

The Secretary said on such matters the President and the Prime Minister should be in touch. However, the question of who initiates military activities is important. The Soviets will support the Arabs if they are attacked. An Arab onslaught on Israel would create a different situation from that of an Israeli attack on the Arabs. This is a most important consideration for the Congress. Israel should weigh heavily any decision to attack.

Ambassador Harman said that those responsible for the destiny of Israel will not be prepared for any deal or a "Munich". Israel is prepared to face the present danger and would prefer to face it than to have its security slowly eroded. Israel understands the importance of who fires the first shot, but does Israel have to accept 10,000 casualties before the U.S. will agree that aggression has occurred? Aggression exists in the build-up of forces on all of Israel's borders, the blockade of the Strait of Tiran, and the belligerent statements threatening the extinction

181

of Israel. In the context of President Kennedy's statement of May 8, 1963, the aggression is already mounted.

The Secretary said that there is some difference between what is said and what is actually done.

The Secretary said that no one can say what the Soviets will do in the event of hostilities. However, if a Jihad mentality is evoked by the Arabs and the Arabs don't attack, how long can this state be maintained. A stalemate could work against Nasser.

Mr. Evron replied that a military build-up sets in motion a chain of events that probably will lead to military action.

The Secretary said we have been told categorically that Egypt will not attack. If we had these assurance from the Soviets in connection with our own security, the U.S. would not rush into a confrontation.

Ambassador Harman said the Soviets were a different people from the Arabs. The Soviets played a rational form of brinkmanship. In answer to the Secretary's question as to how much influence the Soviets actually wielded in Cairo, Ambassador Harman said that this was a weakness on the Soviet side through which their restraint could be neutralized. Nasser's momentum is such that Israel's assumption is that he must be in deadly earnest.

Had Israel acted on May 23 against the advice received from the U.S., Israel would be facing a different political and military situation from that faced today. Israel was at a disadvantage.

The Secretary said that Nasser was sending former Prime Minister and Vice President Zakariyah Muhi ad-Din to Washington this week end. If he should say anything significant, we would let Israel know.

Ambassador Harman said Soviet moves now seemed directed toward gaining time and confirming the new status quo. Israel had a strong feeling that the Soviets would not seek a confrontation with the U.S. in the Middle East. The gut question in Israel is what would the U.S. do to help Israel?

The Secretary said this depends in part on who initiates hostilities. Ambassador Harman questioned what this meant. What does Israel have to take in a situation where she is threatened not with aggression but with genocide? Egypt's action in closing the Strait is a clear act of aggression. Israel was convinced that an attack was inevitable. Nasser has cast himself in a certain role, and now there is no room for any other course of action. If he is challenged quickly and strongly, this might prevent inflation of the conflict. Since May 16, Nasser has shown how he can make rapid moves. Israel operates from five airfields. This question is foremost in Israel's mind. Air power is decisive. If Israel loses initially, Israel has had it. There will be little to salvage. This situation can arise any time. Israel did not agree with the estimate given by Mr. McNamara and General Wheeler that it could absorb a first strike. Israel is not seeking hostilities, but Nasser seems to be playing "for broke". The situation calls for speedy action. The farce in the Security Council must be broken up.

The Secretary said that there were some advantages to Security Council considerations. The fact that the Cuban problem was in the Security Council didn't affect the settlement, but it did allow some prestige to be salvaged which weighed in the settlement.

Ambassador Harman said the test of the Strait must be made in the course of next week. Secretary Rusk replied that the test would take place seven to nine days after a decision was reached. Ambassador Harman said that any testing must include an Israeli flagship. They had one, the Dolphin (ex-Arion)/3/ in Massawa ready to go.

/3/According to a telegraphic summary of the conversation, the Dolphin was formerly the Greek-owned Arion. (Telegram 207977 to Tel Aviv, June 3; National Archives and Records Administration, RG 59, Central Files 1967-69, POL ARAB-ISR)

The Secretary said that John Finney and Chalmers Roberts do not speak for the USG. What the Prime Minister and the President say to each other is the important factor. Ambassador Harman said the public in Israel lives on the *New York Times* and the *Washington Post*.

The Ambassador said he expected to return by Sunday/4/ evening.

/4/June 4.

**133. Telegram From the Embassy in France to the Department of State/1/**

Paris, June 2, 1967, 1910Z.

## Deadly Dogma:
### How Neoconservatives Broke the Law to Deceive America

/1/Source: National Archives and Records Administration, RG 59, Central Files 1967-69, POL ARAB-ISR. Secret; Immediate; Nodis. Received at 4:46 p.m.

19777. Ref: State 206658./2/ I saw Couve de Murville this afternoon at 5:00 o'clock for about half an hour.

/2/In telegram 206658 to Paris, June 1, Rusk asked Bohlen to see Couve de Murville as soon as possible to review the British proposal for a Maritime Declaration and to urge French cooperation. (Ibid.)

1. Couve was in complete agreement with our assumption that war in the Middle East would be disastrous. He also agreed that the Israelis consider the blockade of the Gulf of Aqaba a matter of the highest national importance. He also agreed that the Soviets' behavior is far from clear and did not question my statement that they had not shown any inclination to act responsibly in the present crisis. He said that when the Soviets gave their refusal to French suggestion of a four power get together last Sunday/3/ night it had been couched in very courteous way but did not appear to be categoric in its refusal. He said it was impossible to determine exactly what had started this crisis and did not completely exclude an element of Soviet responsibility, but said that this had been bypassed by events. He agreed however that the ultimate Soviet objective was to reduce Western influence in the Middle East and substitute therefor Soviet influence.

/3/May 28.

2. Couve then said that he would give me what he had just said this afternoon to the Israeli Ambassador, which he thought fully reflected present French attitude toward the situation [in] the Middle East. It follows:

Soviet attitude still uncertain although there had been some indications in New York from Fedorenko of his desire to maintain contact individually with Western powers and that Fedorenko showed no desire to poison the atmosphere. He said he had told Eytan that there were essentially only two solutions to the present state of affairs in the Middle East. One was to go to war, which he impressed on Eytan would be folly since even if Israel scored a military victory it would certainly not lay any groundwork for the future which must in some form or other and at some time or other include accommodation between the Arab states and Israel. If war is excluded, the only other way was negotiation, which would include not only the question of the Gulf of Aqaba but also other questions of a military nature dealing with terrorism, etc., in the area. He told Eytan if the status of the Gulf of Aqaba is discussed neither side will get one hundred percent of what they want and compromise would probably be necessary and to the French Government this should include the normal passage of civilian goods. Couve admitted that the question of the Egyptian attitude towards POL as to whether or not it is a strategic cargo remains unclear and would obviously be a subject of discussion. Eytan asked how could any negotiations take place, to which Couve had replied that it was obviously not possible at the present juncture to have direct Arab/Israeli discussions but there were many other intermediaries, including the great powers. He said he had taken the liberty of mentioning to Eytan that he was convinced of the good will of the U.S. but some indication of a comparable attitude was needed from the USSR. Couve said Eytan had made no comment but Couve had emphasized very strongly the point with him that apart from war the only way out was negotiation. Couve then told me that in regard to the Security Council it was quite clear that neither the U.S. resolution nor the Indian (of course Egyptian inspired) had any chance of obtaining the votes ofall members of the Security Council. Therefore, Seydoux had been instructed to point this out to the Council and to suggest the drafting of a resolution which would merely urge calm on the countries directly involved, which conceivably might obtain the support of all members. Couve however admitted that there was as yet no sign that the Russians were willing to meet in a group of four.

I asked Couve (although State 206752/4/ arrived afterwards) what was meant by the statement following the cabinet meeting that the country that fired the first shot would receive no support and no arms from France, and asked him if this meant that stoppage of a ship going into the Gulf of Aqaba would fall within this category. Couve said that if the Egyptians fired on a ship that this would undoubtedly fall within the terms of the declaration but was not clear at all as to whether or not a forceable stoppage of a ship by the Egyptians would be so considered. In fact, he said that in his view it was the height of prudence to avoid the passage of any ships through the Straits of Tiran for the immediate future.

/4/Telegram 206752 to Paris, June 2, noted that news reports were quoting a comment by French President De Gaulle concerning the Middle East to the effect that whoever shot first would not have French support and asked the Embassy to check on the accuracy of the statement and its meaning. (National Archives and Records Administration, RG 59, Central Files 1967-69, POL ARAB-ISR)

3. Couve said the statement issued after the cabinet meeting this morning set forth France's opinion towards the Maritime Declaration. He said France did not consider this a good idea at the present time

and was therefore not "a partisan" thereof. In reply to my question he said it was not an absolute flat refusal but a disinclination to go along with it at present.

*Comment:* Couve's general attitude showed that French position had not really changed since the beginning of this crisis; that they still are hopeful that the Soviets will change their negative attitude and be willing to join in some form of negotiations and that through these negotiations there might be some arrangement made which would cover the passage of cargo of a non-strategic value, particularly POL through the Straits. He showed no willingness at all to consider the issuance of a Maritime Declaration and certainly none to even contemplate the action in the event it was rejected.

Bohlen

**134. Telegram From the Embassy in the United Arab Republic to the Department of State/1/**

Cairo, June 2, 1967, 2029Z.

/1/Source: National Archives and Records Administration, Central Files 1967-69, POL ARAB-ISR. Secret; Immediate; Nodis. Received at 6:20 p.m. A copy was sent to the President on June 3 with a note from Walt Rostow calling Nasser's response "quite uncompromising," noting that Nasser was willing to receive Vice President Humphrey or to send Vice President Mohieddin to Washington, and stating that he and Rusk agreed that "we should proceed to get Mohieddin here." (Johnson Library, National Security File, Country File, Middle East Crisis)

8397. 1. Following is text UAR Foreign Office "unofficial translation" of letter to President Johnson from President Gamal Abdul Nasser. With reference penultimate paragraph, was explicitly assured by Foreign Minister Riad that it was up to President Johnson to decide whether to send Vice President Humphrey here or invite Vice President Mohieddin to go to Washington, with no expression of UARG preference./2/ While waiting for typing to be completed, enjoyed long pleasant conversation Foreign Minister Riad on non-political matters. Will pouch original letter in Arabic and Foreign Office translation. Text follows:

/2/Telegram 207861 to Cairo, June 3, states that the President would welcome a visit from Mohieddin and that in view of the urgency of the situation, "we hope it will be possible for him to come without delay." It states that, if asked, Nolte could say that a corresponding visit to Cairo by a "very senior representative of the President" would be sympathetically considered if both Presidents decided such a step could be useful. It states that Harman had been informed about the possibility of the visit. (National Archives and Records Administration, RG 59, Central Files 1967-69, POL ARAB-ISR)

2. Cairo, June 2, 1967. Dear President,

3. I welcome your initiative in writing to me on the current situation in the Arab homeland. For however distant the point of agreement between us seems from the scope of our outlook at the present stage, I am convinced that any joint endeavor on our part to establish communication of thought, might at least contribute to dissipate part of the artificial clouds intended to depict the exercise of right as a sin and the right of defense as aggression.

4. It would be useful in the assessment of current events, to view them in their chronological and logical entity, to avoid misunderstanding and make a sound, reasonable, and fair evaluation of the facts we face.

5. Hence, I shall try to set forth a number of facts which I would term as preliminary:

6. First: It is essential that we go back to the few days which preceded the measures which the United Arab Republic took of late, and to recall the dangerously aggressive situation created by the Israeli authorities vis-a-vis the Syrian Arab Republic, the hostile threats proclaimed by a number of Israeli leaders, and the accompanying mass troop concentrations on the Syrian border in preparation for an imminent aggression on Syria. It was only natural then, that the United Arab Republic should assume her responsibilities and take all measures necessary for defense and to deter the planned aggression against our countries.

7. Second: Defense measures taken by the United Arab Republic made it imperative that our armed forces move to their advanced positions on the border to be able to cope with developments and through their very presence foil Israel's premeditated invasion. Urged by our concern for the United Nations Emergency Forces, we found it imperative that they should withdraw: such has become our final position on the matter.

8. Third: Following the withdrawal of the UNEF, it was only logical that the United Arab Republic armed forces should occupy their positions, among which was the area of Sharm el Sheikh overlooking the Straits of Tiran. It was equally logical that we exercise our established sovereign rights on the Straits and on our territorial waters in the Gulf.

9. Here again, I wish to take you a few years back to the tripartite aggression on Egypt: We still recall with appreciation, the fair position adopted by your country with regard to that aggression.

10. Prior to the aggression, the United Arab Republic exercised its established legal rights with regard to Israeli shipping in the Straits and the Gulf. These rights are indisputable. Following the departure of the United Nations Emergency Forces and their replacement by our armed forces in the area, it was unthinkable that Israeli shipping or strategic materials destined for Israel be allowed passage. Our position thereon, in addition to Ily being legitimately established, it indeed aims at removing the last vestige of the tripartite aggression, in consonance with the moral principle which rules that no aggressor be rewarded for his aggression.

11. In all the measures we have adopted in defense of our land and our rights, we have underlined two points:

12. First: That we shall defend ourselves against any aggression, with all our means and potentialities

13. Second: That we shall continue to allow innocent passage of foreign shipping in our territorial waters.

14. These are facts relevant to the direct position proclaimed by the United Arab Republic, and which we feel afford no ground for some to create a climate of crisis or to launch that psychological campaign against us.

15. While this campaign takes on new dimensions and forms we notice complete and regrettable overlooking of a number of other facts which I wish to term as basic. These are the very facts which carry full weight on current events and will continue to have their bearing on the future until all appreciate fully and assess their dimensions and roots. Here I shall refer to two facts:

16. First: The rights of the Arab people of Palestine. In our view, this is the most important fact that should be recognized. An aggressive

armed force was able to oust that people from their country and reduce them to refugees on the borders of their homeland.

17. Today the forces of aggression impede the Arab people's established right of return and life in their homeland, despite the UN resolutions, the last of which was adopted last year.

18. The second fact is related to Israel's position towards the Armistice Agreements: a position represented not merely by the constant violation of those agreements, but which has gone as far as to deny their presence and refuse to adhere to them. It has even gone as far as to occupy the demilitarized zones, oust the UN observers and insult the international organization and its flag.

19. Those are two basic facts which should be considered in the assessment of today's events and developments.

20. In your message you referred to two points:

21. First: you urge that we put the past aside and endeavor to rescue the Middle East or rather the whole human community through the avoidance of hostilities. Here, allow me to refer to the policy of the United Arab Republic which does not restrict herself to placing world peace as an objective, but goes beyond that and assumes a positive role on which I do not wish to elaborate lest I should border on the area of self-glorification. As for endeavors to avoid military operations, I have but to emphasize what I have already declared that the measures we have adopted were imposed by the forces of aggression and their conceit as well as by their belief that they have reached the stage where they could impose their aggressive policy. Yet, our forces have not initiated any aggressive act, but no doubt, we shall resist with all our potentialities any aggression launched against us or against any Arab state.

22. Second: Your observation that the conflicts of our time cannot be solved by the crossings of frontiers with arms and men. Here, I share your view. Yet, we have to see how this principle is applied to every case. If you are referring to the crossing of the demarcation lines by some individuals of the Palestinian people I would urge the importance of considering this aspect in the general perspective of the question of Palestine. Here also, I may ask how far any government is able to control the feelings of more than one million Palestinians who, for twenty years, the international community--whose responsibility herein is inescapable--has failed to secure their return to their homeland. The UN General Assembly merely confirms that right at every session. The crossing of the demarcation lines by some Palestinian individual is, in

point of fact, merely a manifestation of anger by which those people are naturally possessed as they meet with the full denial of their rights by the international community, and by the powers which side with Israel and assist it materially and morally.

23. Whatever our attempts to divide the aspects of the problem, it is imperative in the end that we return to its origin and fundamentals, namely the right of Palestinian people to return to their homeland, and the responsibility of the international community in securing them the exercise of this right.

24. My letter may seem rather long in a way: Yet, it was my wish to explain briefly some of the basic features of the situation we now face in the Arab region.

25. Finally, I wish to assure you that we would welcome listening to Mr. Hubert Humphrey, the United States Vice President, at anytime he may choose to visit the UAR. We shall provide him with a picture of the situation as we conceive it amidst the fundamental events faced by the Arab nation today. I am ready to send Vice President Zakareya Mohieddin, to Washington immediately to meet with you and expound our viewpoint.

26. Please accept my regards and considerations.

27. (Sgd) (Gamal Abdel Nasser) President of the United Arab Republic.

Nolte

### 135. Memorandum From Director of Central Intelligence Helms to President Johnson

Washington, June 2, 1967.

[Source: Johnson Library, National Security File, Country File, Middle East Crisis, Vol. III. Secret; Sensitive. 5 pages of source text not declassified.]

### 136. Memorandum From Nathaniel Davis of the National Security Council Staff to the President's Special Assistant (Rostow)/1/

Washington, June 2, 1967.

# Appendix B: Arab-Israeli Crisis and War, 1967

/1/Source: Johnson Library, National Security File, Country File, Middle East Crisis, Vol. III. Top Secret; Nodis.

SUBJECT
A Scenario of the Soviet Role

From the bits and pieces of Intelligence we have been receiving on the Soviet role in this crisis, it might be useful to set down the following "scenario." It's a guess, but I think it is about as probable as any other hypothesis.

The understandings reached during Gromyko's trip in late March were probably general in nature, and not an "attack plan."

In early May, it is probable that Soviet agents actually picked up intelligence reports of a planned Israeli raid into Syria. I would not be surprised if the reports were at least partly true. The Israeli have made such raids before; they have been under heavy provocation; and they maintain pretty good security (so we might well not know about a planned raid).

Intelligence being an uncertain business, the Soviet agents may not have known the scale of the raid and may have exaggerated its scope and purpose.

Apparently the Soviets warned the Syrians. Whether they deliberately magnified the threat is hard to say. They bear neither the Israeli nor ourselves any great love, and there may well have been some element of deliberate exaggeration. However, this was not necessarily a calculated incitement to conflict--made out of whole cloth and responsive to a global design. The Soviets did accompany their warnings of Israeli action with advice toward restraint.

The Syrians and the UAR were also quite ready to exaggerate what the Soviets said and feed on their own fears and ambitions.

There is still no evidence that Nasser consulted with the Soviets or got their agreement to close the straits. In fact, the Soviets have still taken no position on the straits issue.

Like everybody else, the Soviets know that Nasser is two strikes ahead--with the withdrawal of UNEF and the strait now effectively closed for almost two weeks. They are in a position where it is extremely difficult to back out of a position of supporting their friends across the board. Whatever the situation before, they have the strongest interest in maintaining the status quo and consolidating the victory. About the only negative influence from the point of view of their self-interest is the danger that things will really get out of hand. However, they increasingly realize how close to out-of-hand things are. We understand from New York that Fedorenko now is taking things more seriously.

I doubt that the Soviets are much more confident than we are in their ability to call the shots and control their friends. That's not very confident.

N.D.

**137. Memorandum From the Deputy Assistant Secretary of Defense for International Security Affairs (Hoopes) to Secretary of Defense McNamara/1/**

I-23411/67

Washington, June 2, 1967.

/1/Source: Washington National Records Center, OSD Files: FRC 330 72 A 2468, Middle East, 381.3. Secret; No Release. A stamped notation on the memorandum, dated June 14, indicates that McNamara saw it.

SUBJECT
Middle East Situation

Attached is the paper on the question of tailoring the traffic pattern in the Strait of Tiran./2/ This was addressed by the Control Group (Rostow, Vance, Kohler) yesterday evening. I sent you a copy earlier yesterday, but I feel it is now important (following our telephone conversation of this morning) to re-emphasize several significant points in it.

/2/The attachment, a June 1 memorandum from Hoopes to the Middle East Control Group, recorded a May 31 meeting of the Military Contingency Working Group that considered the feasibility of testing the UAR blockade by unescorted ships. The working group also decided to continue military supply shipments to Near East countries under existing commitments, but to make no new commitments. A copy of Hoopes' memorandum is in the National Archives and Records

## Appendix B: Arab-Israeli Crisis and War, 1967

Administration, RG 59, Office of the Executive Secretariat, Middle East Crisis Files, 1967, Entry 5190, Box 18, Control Group Data, Vol. I, Folder 1.

As indicated on page 2, the basic difficulty in organizing a controlled series of probes is the general unavailability of appropriate shipping. Only tankers present a test case, but these will be hard to come by unless the US takes positive action (through charter or other means) to arrange for a group of ships of appropriate registries. The options have been further narrowed by the Israeli position that it cannot permit even the peaceful refusal of an Israeli-owned ship at the Strait without having immediate recourse to military retaliation. Moreover, increasing doubt is being expressed by people like Walter Levy, the reputable oil consultant to the State Department, that the Shah of Iran will be able politically to go on supplying oil to Israel. Levy strongly recommended at the Control Group meeting yesterday evening that we should avoid pressing the Shah to include his oil in a test tanker, but should try to find oil from another source--e.g., Indonesia. This judgment was challenged, and attempts to have Iran stand firm will be quickly made, through Ambassador Meyer in Teheran and through Mr. Harriman (who will see the Shah in Europe over this weekend)./3/ But if Levy is reflecting the political reality in Iran, this would further circumscribe and delay even an unescorted test probe.

/3/For Harriman's conversations with the Shah, see telegrams 19869 and 19914 from Paris, June 5 and 6 in *Foreign Relations*, 1964-1968, vol. XXII, Documents 207 and 208.

I refer you also to page 5 (paragraph 4) and the judgment that even the successful passage of an unescorted US flag tanker would set in motion Cairo's propaganda media, denouncing us as the enemy of the Arabs and as Israel's protector. The CIA judgment (expressed on page 6),/4/ which is addressed to the political consequences of a passage by a ship under US naval escort, is also highly relevant. If true, Nasser could severely damage the United States and West Europe, politically and economically, without firing a shot.

/4/The reference is to a quotation in Hoopes' memorandum from a May 31 CIA report (not found). It estimates that if a U.S. ship were escorted through the Strait of Tiran by a U.S. naval vessel, ignoring all challenges, UAR forces would let them through under protest. It continues: "We do not believe that Cairo wishes to make any direct encounter with US military power. Indeed the UAR may see a US naval challenge of the blockade as serving their interests, as the political consequences of such a move would be far-reaching. The UAR would formally accuse the US of acting as Israel's military ally to commit aggression against the Arabs. It would expand and intensify its propaganda and diplomatic efforts against special US positions throughout the Arab world. In particular it would seek to harass US oil operations and urge the nationalization of US oil properties in Saudi Arabia, Iraq, Kuwait, and Libya. During the present super-heated and emotional climate prevailing in the Arab world, US interests in the area would almost certainly suffer considerably."

I attach particular importance to the conclusion reached by the Working Group (on page 6) that, given the present atmosphere in the Arab world and the effectiveness of Arab and Soviet propaganda, it would not be possible to present a Western blockade running (particularly if armed escort were involved) as simply an assertion of a recognized international right. Those propaganda media would almost certainly succeed in branding the US as the ally and protector of Israel against the Arabs. On this judgment, we could not avoid a damaging political polarization in the event that we organize and attempt to use a naval task force (whether US or multilateral).

One reason why I am pessimistic about the number and quality of likely adherents to a maritime declaration is that many of the potentials are now beginning to believe that even such a declaration on their part would lead to serious discrimination against their Middle Eastern interests by Nasser-directed Arab actions. Their judgment in this respect acknowledges Nasser's political power. As you know, the French are extremely cool to both the declaration and the naval escort, the Canadians have made quite clear that they will not participate in a naval force and that even their adherence to a declaration depends on the adherence of several others and on a "balanced program" designed to resolve the crisis without violence. The British Cabinet gives increasing evidence of softening its position, as it contemplates the UK's severe economic vulnerabilities in the Middle East (oil revenues, passage through Suez, and the fact that Saudi and Kuwaiti deposits in London represent two-thirds of the UK's sterling balance).

It is increasingly my conviction (as I believe it is Mr. Vance's) that we must put our major efforts into seeking a political settlement based on compromise, and should be extremely cautious about pinning our hopes on a broadly supported maritime declaration and especially about getting publicly committed to a naval escort force. It is possible that the indication in yesterday's Cairo press that oil may not be a "strategic" commodity in the UAR view is an important ingredient of such a political compromise.

A further significant development yesterday was King Hussein's request for the removal of the US training detachment in Jordan, followed almost immediately by his request for the removal of the five

F-104 aircraft./5/ Last evening he also made known his decision to withdraw the Jordanian aviation cadets from the pilot training programs in the US. The full implications of these acts are not yet clear, but it does seem evident that Nasser has required him at least to delimit sharply his politico-military relations with the US as a condition of their new defense pact. UAR-Jordan amity remains, however, very fragile.

/5/In a meeting with Ambassador Burns on May 31, King Hussein requested withdrawal of a small USAF detachment stationed in Jordan to provide training on F-104 aircraft to Jordanian pilots. Burns reported the meeting in telegram 3929 from Amman (cited in footnote 2, Document 107). Circular telegram 206650, June 1, states that the Jordanian Government had requested withdrawal of the USAF aircraft as well. (National Archives and Records Administration, RG 59, Central Files 1967-69, POL ARAB-ISR) The USAF personnel and aircraft were in Jordan to provide training to Jordanian pilots for 18 F-104 aircraft Jordan was purchasing, which were scheduled to begin arriving in July 1967. See *Foreign Relations*, 1964-1968, vol. XVIII, Document 373, footnote 3.

Townsend Hoopes

### 138. President's Daily Brief

Washington, June 3, 1967.

[Source: Johnson Library, National Security File, NSC Histories, Middle East Crisis, Vol. 6, Appendix A. Top Secret; [*codeword not declassified*]. 1 page of source text not declassified.]

### 139. Letter From President Johnson to Prime Minister Eshkol/1/

Washington, June 3, 1967.

/1/Source: Johnson Library, National Security File, Country File, Middle East Crisis, Vol. III. Secret. Rostow sent a draft letter, drafted by Battle and Sisco, with his handwritten revisions to the President at 7:25 p.m. on June 2. Johnson marked his approval on Rostow's covering memorandum. (Ibid.) Rostow sent him the letter for signature with a covering memorandum on June 3 at 2:50 p.m., noting that he understood Johnson wanted to read it again before it was sent and adding, "It may be urgent that we put this letter on record soon." (Ibid.)

# Deadly Dogma:
## How Neoconservatives Broke the Law to Deceive America

The final letter includes additional revisions, which, according to a handwritten note by Harold H. Saunders, were given to him by the President on the telephone on the afternoon of June 3. (Ibid., NSC Histories, Middle East Crisis) A copy of the draft with Saunders' handwritten revisions is filed ibid., Memos to the President, Walt Rostow, Vol. 30. A handwritten note on the letter states that it was sent to the Department of State at 4:30 p.m.

Dear Mr. Prime Minister:

I am grateful for your letter of May 30./2/ I appreciate particularly the steadfastness with which the Government and people of Israel have maintained a posture of resolution and calm in a situation of grave tension. All of us understand how fateful the steps we take may be. I hope we can continue to move firmly and calmly toward a satisfactory solution.

/2/See Document 102.

Our position in this crisis rests on two principles which are vital national interests of the United States. The first is that we support the territorial integrity and political independence of all of the countries of the Middle East. This principle has now been affirmed by four American Presidents. The second is our defense of the basic interest of the entire world community in the freedom of the seas. As a leading maritime nation, we have a vital interest in upholding freedom of the seas, and the right of passage through straits of an international character.

As you know, the United States considers the Gulf of Aqaba to be an international waterway and believes that the entire international maritime community has a substantial interest in assuring that the right of passage through the Strait of Tiran and Gulf is maintained.

I am sure Foreign Minister Eban has reported to you the written statement which I had prepared and from which Ambassador Harman made notes during our meeting of May 26./3/ The full text of that statement is as follows:

/3/See Document 77.

"The United States has its own constitutional processes which are basic to its action on matters involving war and peace. The Secretary General has not yet reported to the UN Security Council and the

Council has not yet demonstrated what it may or may not be able or willing to do although the United States will press for prompt action in the UN.

"I have already publicly stated this week our views on the safety of Israel and on the Strait of Tiran. Regarding the Strait, we plan to pursue vigorously the measures which can be taken by maritime nations to assure that the Strait and Gulf remain open to free and innocent passage of the vessels of all nations.

"I must emphasize the necessity for Israel not to make itself responsible for the initiation of hostilities. Israel will not be alone unless it decides to go alone. We cannot imagine that it will make this decision."

I explained to Mr. Eban, I want to protect the territorial integrity of Israel and other nations in that area of the world and will provide as effective American support as possible to preserve the peace and freedom of your nation and of the area./4/ I stressed too the need to act in concert with other nations, particularly those with strong maritime interests. As you will understand and as I explained to Mr. Eban, it would be unwise as well as most unproductive for me to act without the full consultation and backing of Congress. We are now in the process of urgently consulting the leaders of our Congress and counseling with its membership./5/

/4/Before Saunders added Johnson's revisions, the first two sentences of this paragraph read: I told Mr. Eban I could not foresee then, and I cannot now foresee, the specific steps which may prove desirable and necessary. I explained that I want to do everything I can to provide Israel with effective American support."

/5/Before Saunders added Johnson's revisions, the last two sentences of this paragraph read: "And, as you will understand, I cannot act at all without full backing of Congress. I am now in the process of urgently consulting the leaders of our Congress."

We are now engaged in doing everything we can through the United Nations. We recognize the difficulties of securing constructive action in the Security Council, but we are convinced that the world organization, which for the past decade has played a major role in the Middle East, must make a real effort to discharge its responsibilities for the maintenance of peace.

## Deadly Dogma:
## *How Neoconservatives Broke the Law to Deceive America*

We are moving ahead in our diplomatic efforts, in concert with the United Kingdom and with your diplomatic representatives, to secure a declaration by the principal maritime powers asserting the right of passage through the Strait and Gulf. A copy of this declaration has been given to your Ambassador. Such a declaration could be an important step both in relation to the proceedings in the Security Council and also in the event those proceedings do not lead to a successful outcome.

We are also exploring on an urgent basis the British suggestion for the establishment of an international naval presence in the area of the Strait of Tiran. As I said to Mr. Eban, there is doubt that a number of other maritime powers would be willing to take steps of this nature unless and until United Nations processes have been exhausted. We must continue our efforts to mobilize international support for this effort. Our leadership is unanimous that the United States should not move in isolation./6/

/6/Before Saunders added Johnson's revisions, the last sentence of this paragraph read: "I would not wish the United States to move in isolation."

On the matter of liaison and communication, I believe our relations can be improved. We have completely and fully exchanged views with General Amit.

We will remain in continuing communication with Ambassador Harman and Minister Evron here in Washington and value greatly the exchanges we are able to have through them with the Government of Israel, as well as through Ambassador Barbour in Tel Aviv.

Sincerely,

Lyndon B. Johnson

### 140. Telegram From the Department of State to the Embassy in Israel/1/

Washington, June 4, 1967, 2:03 p.m.

/1/Source: National Archives and Records Administration, RG 59, Central Files 1967-69, POL ARAB-ISR. Secret; Exdis. Drafted by Battle on June 3 and approved by Rusk.

208004. 1. Secretary called in Israeli Charg☐ to present President Johnson's reply Prime Minister's letter (sent separately)./2/ Noted letter did not attempt repeat everything that had been said previously but was designed summarize where we are at moment. He reviewed current efforts within Security Council and discussions re Maritime Declaration. Then stated U.S. had nothing further on Russian position on important aspects current issues. He asked Eshkol [Evron] whether GOI had info this matter. Eshkol [Evron] replied in negative, indicating, however, he had Eshkol's letter to Kosygin which he would provide us after translation. There were in opinion GOI indications USSR prodding Egyptians but still no reflection their attitude on Straits. It was agreed U.S. and GOI would keep in close touch regarding Russian intentions.

/2/Document 139; the text was transmitted in telegram 207955 to Tel Aviv, June 3, which states that Rusk gave the letter to Evron that afternoon. (National Archives and Records Administration, RG 59, Central Files 1967-69, POL ARAB-ISR) Rusk met with Evron from 5:15 to 5:40 p.m. (Johnson Library, Rusk Appointment Book)

2. Secretary briefed Charge in general terms talks Prime Minister Wilson in which Middle East problems had figured prominently. Clear from these discussions that U.S. and U.K. were mobilizing support on Declaration and considering carefully contingencies that might follow. In addition, U.S. and U.K. looking carefully into economic, financial, and other aspects problem. Clear that U.K. regards matter as serious issue to which it is giving most urgent attention. From U.S. point of view, important question was how involve as many governments as possible in plans for future. Secretary assumed GOI talking to France and Canada. French position at present unsatisfactory which was perhaps not too surprising. One key question was what France would do if merchant vessel transited Straits and UAR fired first shot. De Gaulle statement not precise on point.

3. Evron pressed Secretary re time factors current plans to which Secretary replied U.S. working very hard several tracks. Should know by about Monday what Security Council can do. We are trying speed up consideration Declaration with target for mid-week to know how much support we have. Moreover, Department spending much time with Congressional groups to inform them of situation. So far response in Congress constructive and encouraging but indicates strong feeling U.S. should deal with problem multilaterally.

4. Evron agreed transmit letter Prime Minister soonest.

Rusk

*Deadly Dogma:*
*How Neoconservatives Broke the Law to Deceive America*

**141. Circular Telegram From the Department of State to Arab Capitals/1/**

Washington, June 3, 1967, 7:17 p.m.

/1/Source: National Archives and Records Administration, RG 59, Central Files 1967-69, POL ARAB-ISR. Secret. Drafted and approved by Rusk. Sent to Algiers, Amman, Baghdad, Baida, Beirut, Cairo, Jidda, Kuwait, Rabat, Sanaa, Tel Aviv, and Tunis.

207956. Eyes Only for Ambassador from Secretary.

I wish to express my personal appreciation to our Ambassadors in Arab Capitals for their full and timely reporting and for frank expressions of views on the present situation in the Near East. The considerations which you have advanced are being taken fully into account in a situation which is as complex and as dangerous as any we have faced. I should like to put before you some additional considerations and ask you to put your minds to possible solutions which can prevent war.

1. **You should not assume that the United States can order Israel not to fight for what it considers to be its most vital interests. We have used the utmost restraint and, thus far, have been able to hold Israel back. But the "Holy War" psychology of the Arab world is matched by an apocalyptic psychology within Israel. Israel may make a decision that it must resort to force to protect its vital interests. In dealing with the issues involved, therefore, we must keep in mind the necessity for finding a solution with which Israel can be restrained.**

2. Each side appears to look with relative equanimity upon the prospect of major hostilities and each side apparently is confident of success. Which estimate is correct cannot be fully known unless tested by the event but someone is making a major miscalculation. It does not help that Israel believes that time is working against them because of the continuing Arab build-up and deployment of forces. If anything could be done in the direction of reversing the mobilization on both sides, this would, of course, be a great advantage.

3. You should bear in mind the background of the application of the statement of four American Presidents that (to quote from President Johnson's statement of May 23) "The United States is firmly committed to the support of the political independence and territorial integrity of all the nations of that area." You will recall the actions taken by the

## Appendix B: Arab-Israeli Crisis and War, 1967

Eisenhower Administration when Egypt was attacked by Israel, Britain and France and when Lebanon was seriously threatened by Syria. You will recall our steady and substantial support to Jordan to reinforce its position over and against Egypt. You will recall that President Kennedy sent a squadron of U.S. fighters to Saudi Arabia as a demonstration of support when Saudi Arabia was being threatened by Egypt. Most of you may know that we used a major diplomatic effort in Cairo to cool off subversive and propaganda assaults upon Libya. We supported Algeria's demand for independence and have tried to steady the nerves of Tunisia and Morocco when they felt threatened by Algeria. When Israel has been attacked by terrorist groups we have supported Israel; when Israel resorted to disproportionate actions of retaliation against Samu in Jordan, we publicly and privately censored Israel in the strongest terms. I suggest we have a strong case for the idea that we have been even-handed with respect to the political independence and territorial integrity of Near Eastern countries.

A major issue for us in this present crisis involves the commitments we made at the time of the wind-up of the Suez affair. At that time we were acting on behalf of Egypt. As a part of the settlement which obtained the withdrawal of Israeli forces from the Sinai, including Sharm el Sheikh, we assured Israel that we would support an international right of passage through the Strait of Tiran. We endorsed Israel's statement in the General Assembly (in fact it was drafted in consultation with Secretary Dulles) that Israel would have the right under Article 51 of the Charter to protect its flagships transiting that Strait if fired upon. Egypt was aware of these positions and, although it did not endorse them at the time, it was the beneficiary of the arrangements made.

4. The central principle of international law involved in the Strait of Tiran was encompassed in the Conventions on the law of the sea of 1958. This principle is of vital importance to us all over the world where there are many such narrow passages connecting bodies of international waters. In any event, the United States has given some pledges on the matter and we must give the most sober attention to all the implications of such pledges and any failure on our part to insist upon them.

5. There may be some flexibility in what Cairo would be willing to do before major hostilities. The Strait of Tiran is a key issue. The free passage of crude oil is a major part of that issue. We shall not know details until further explorations of the problem with Cairo or intermediaries. We cannot abandon, in principle, the right of Israeli flagships to transit the Strait. There might be some possibility of a breathing space if in fact passage were permitted for genuinely peaceful traffic, including crude oil. This is not a proposal on our side

but an indication of a possible de facto standstill pending further diplomatic effort.

6. I have presented these considerations in order to enlist the best thought of our Ambassadors in Arab Capitals as to profitable approaches to the problem. It will do no good to ask Israel simply to accept the present status quo in the Strait because Israel will fight and we could not restrain her. We cannot throw up our hands and say that, in that event, let them fight while we try to remain neutral. I should be glad to have any further suggestions any of you might have on this situation.

Rusk

**142. Memorandum From Robert N. Ginsburgh of the National Security Council Staff to the President's Special Assistant (Rostow)/1/**

Washington, June 3, 1967.

/1/Source: Johnson Library, National Security File, Country File, Middle East Crisis, Situation Reports. Top Secret; [*codeword not declassified*].

SUBJECT
Who Would Win a War? Israel or the UAR

1. The attached document/2/--prepared a week ago--is the best I have seen on comparing the military capabilities of Israel and the UAR. I suggest you read all of it.

/2/The attachment is apparently a draft of Document 76.

2. It concludes:

--Israel could get air supremacy over the Sinai in one to three days-- depending on who struck first.

--Israel would lose a third to half of its air force. (This estimate may be high; one-fourth to one-third losses might be closer to the mark.)

--Israel would drive the Egyptians west of the Suez Canal in seven to nine days.

--Israel could contain any attacks by Syria or Jordan during this period.

3. Since this was written, the UAR has gained a number of military benefits:

--The UAR has consolidated positions in Sinai.
--The UAR has manned the Straits of Aqaba.
--The UAR has mined certain areas.
--Arab command, control, and planning has probably improved.
--The threat to Israel posed by Jordan has increased.
--UAR logistics in the Sinai have probably improved.

4. By a delay of one week--28 May to 4 June--the Arabs have made a net military gain if war should now occur. The ultimate outcome--according to "my experts"--would be unchanged. Israel would still win, but

--It *might* take 8-10 days to drive to the Suez.
--Israel *might* suffer 5-10% more casualties.

5. If war outbreak were delayed one more week--to 11 June, the Israeli military position would probably deteriorate further--but at a slower rate. "My experts" judge that:

Israel would still win, but

--It *might* take as much as 9 days to two weeks.
--Israelis *might* suffer an additional 5% casualties.

6. After 11 June, the military balance would not change until the economic effects of mobilization began to affect military posture.

7. Some of my experts think that the above underrates Israel. I suspect that if I were a responsible Israeli commander, I might be less sanguine even though I had no doubt about the ultimate military outcome. The only other nagging doubt is that sometimes in the past professional military opinion has been awfully wrong, but I can find no objective basis to challenge the present estimate.

8. Thus, I conclude that Israeli concern about delaying a war which they fear is inevitable is based primarily on their concern about a deterioration in their political and diplomatic position rather than on military factors.

G

**143. Intelligence Memorandum Prepared in the Central Intelligence Agency/1/**

[*document number not declassified*]

Washington, June 3, 1967.

/1/Source: Johnson Library, National Security File, Country File, Middle East Crisis, CIA Intelligence Memoranda, 5/67-7/67. Top Secret; [*codeword not declassified*]. Prepared in the Central Intelligence Agency's Directorate of Intelligence.

THE CURRENT FOCUS OF THE NEAR EAST CRISIS

Summary

Reporting during the past few days has focused on two primary aspects of the Near East crisis. One is the rapidly growing belief in Israel that time is running out, and that if Israel is not to suffer an ultimately fatal defeat it must very soon either strike or obtain absolutely iron-clad security assurances from the West. The second aspect is the rise of a euphoric, band-wagon spirit among the Arab States, leading even moderate Arabs to believe that the time may in fact have come when the Arabs can close in on Israel with some hope of success. There are in addition a number of reports indicating that anti-US actions are being planned, to be put in motion if the US moves to frustrate what the Arabs now tend to see as a "victory."

1. All reporting from Israel shows mounting pressure for a "decision." The popular applause greeting General Moshe Dayan's appointment as defense minister--"go, go Moshe"--indicates that the mood is strongly "action." Dayan's appointment should assure that the "hawks" accept decisions of the coalition government more readily than they otherwise would, but it also indicates that Prime Minister Eshkol has suffered a setback and must adapt his policy to the views of the tough-minded military whom Dayan represents.

2. The Israeli military, [*1 line of source text not declassified*], have already shown apprehension over the consequences of extended delay. The Egyptians have been permitted to make an orderly build-up of ground forces in Sinai, moving aircraft to advanced fields and setting up at least the rudiments of an air defense system there. The Israeli

strategy calls for gaining control of the air as the first essential step in the campaign. Although all reports indicate that the Israelis are still confident of victory, they are increasingly nervous about the cost, and, even more important, about the possibility that the Egyptians may somehow get in an initial air strike on Israeli cities or air fields. The Israeli "hawks" may fear that such a strike would do significant psychological damage to the affluent Israeli society, even if it did not have much material effect.

3. The Arabs are sniffing blood. So fast and far does Nasir's bandwagon seem to be rolling that even the Iranian government, long friendly to Israel and bitterly hostile to Nasir, has been compelled to issue a statement mouthing phrases about Muslim solidarity. Tunisian President Bourguiba, the only "Arab" leader in recent years to suggest publicly some modus vivendi with Israel, has also had his government say that it stands behind, though evidently not with, Nasir.

4. The Arabs evidently expect that the US and the UK will come to Israel's rescue, and are doing some planning for this eventuality. Their view of US and British policy is being fed by a stream of "intelligence" reports--e.g., that US airborne brigades in West Germany are on alert; "confirmed" information that Wheelus Field is being used to ship US arms to Israel; that British, French, and US airmen have arrived in Israel; that Israeli rockets have been stationed at Eilat under US instructions.

5. The range of Arab reaction in the event of US and UK intervention, or indeed before such a development, is indicated not only by public threats to close up the Suez Canal, to destroy Western oil assets, etc., but also by some specific preparations. [*4 lines of source text not declassified*] Terrorist bombing against US offices in Saudi Arabia was resumed on 2 June. Meanwhile, the US Embassy in Kuwait has reported that it assesses the possibility of an oil shutdown there as more real than it had been earlier in the crisis. In Libya, the present mood is that the US base at Wheelus would be closed.

6. Although the tenor of many of the anti-US pronouncements suggests that they are being issued more to head off pro-Nasir pressures than to express actual intentions, there seems to be a real danger in the cumulative effect of the threats. In countries where there are obvious and available targets other than oil or military installations--e.g., the American University of Beirut, US or UK airline and branch bank offices--these might be subjected to direct attack even before Arab governments moved in on oil or base installations where their own interests are more heavily engaged.

7. In less tangible terms, the damage to the US position in the area already appears serious. During the past twenty years, a generation of Arab youth have grown to maturity under bombardment of the idea that Israel would not exist if the US had not created it. This conviction is hardening, and is reflected in the new, rude frankness with which Arab leaders talk to our representatives, as well as in such out-of-the-way items as a Sudanese editorial calling for local enforcement of the Arab boycott against Ford and Coca Cola. These things are not serious in themselves--and some of the editorials and demonstrations are no doubt paid for by the Egyptians or Soviets--but they are pointers of the way in which minds are moving as the crisis deepens.

8. Nor are hardening attitudes toward the US limited to the Arabs. In Israel, particularly among the hawks, there is a rising chorus of sentiment which sees Washington as holding Israel back and thereby selling the Israelis out. This is the other side of the general belief in Israel that only the Israelis really know how to deal with the Arabs and could do so successfully were it not for US pressures.

**144. Memorandum From the President's Special Assistant (Rostow) to President Johnson/1/**

Washington, June 4, 1967, 11:30 a.m.

/1/Source: Johnson Library, National Security File, Country File, Middle East Crisis, Vol. III. Secret. Rostow sent copies to Rusk and McNamara.

Mr. President:

The purpose of this memorandum is to lay out a course of action for the coming week (or two weeks) which will maximize the chance that we can: (1) achieve our objectives in the Middle East without an Arab-Israeli war; and (2) should such an Arab-Israeli war come about, produce minimum damage to the U.S. position in the world and to our position in our own country, including continued support for the war in Viet Nam.

*I. The Situation.*

It is now increasingly clear that the Israelis will wait only about a week to take on themselves the forcing of the blockade at the Gulf of Aqaba.

# Appendix B: Arab-Israeli Crisis and War, 1967

They clearly envisage forcing Nasser to fire the first shot; they will respond on a limited basis in Sinai but be prepared to fight a war against all the Arab forces arrayed against them without external assistance in manpower or other direct application of foreign military force.

The plan for an international regatta to force, say, an oil ship through the Straits is unlikely to get operational support except for four countries: the U.S., the U.K., Australia, and Netherlands.

The moderate Arabs--and, in fact, virtually all Arabs who fear the rise of Nasser as a result of this crisis--would prefer to have him cut down by the Israelis rather than by external forces.

Beyond these factors the situation in the Middle East is that the radical nationalism represented by Nasser, while powerful at the moment in the wake of his breakthrough against U Thant, is waning: Arab socialism and other such doctrines have not proved successful; the moderates of the region (Turkey, Iran, Jordan, Saudi Arabia, Lebanon) have done better than Egypt, Syria, and Iraq; Nasser's plans for external expansion have not gone well; in short, we are dealing with Nasser not on a rising trend but in somewhat the same as Khrushchev in the Cuba missile crisis; Nasser is trying to achieve a quick fix against an underlying waning position.

Just beneath the surface is the potentiality for a new phase in the Middle East of moderation; a focusing on economic development; regional collaboration; and an acceptance of Israel as part of the Middle East if a solution to the refugee problem can be found. But all this depends on Nasser's being cut down to size.

The problem before us is whether this crisis can be surmounted in ways which lead on to that historical transition and which avoid: the destruction of Israel, on the one hand, or the crystallization of a bloc unified only by a hostility to Israel, which would require us to maintain Israel as a kind of Hong Kong enclave in the region.

## II. The Israeli Case for Unilateral Action.

The Israelis believe that their long-run future in the area--including the Arab mentality--requires that they solve the problem before them on their own. They wish in the end to be part of the Middle East. They feel that dealing with this situation on their own is necessary to achieve not merely self-respect but respect in the region.

### *Deadly Dogma:*
### *How Neoconservatives Broke the Law to Deceive America*

They believe taking on the blockade themselves will make it easier for the United States to support them in other ways, short of troops. They believe it easier for the U.S. to honor its commitment of 1957 to recognize the legitimacy of their forcing the blockade than to mobilize on an international basis an effective U.S. and international commitment to use force to break the blockade. Their own diplomatic soundings, like ours, make clear how small the party would be prepared to use force to assert the international interests in the Gulf of Aqaba, including Israeli interests.

They perceive that the USSR is less likely to intervene with military force if they take on Nasser than for U.S. and a few friends to take on Nasser on the Aqaba issue; and they judge it would be better for U. S.-Arab relations in the long run, but also in terms of Western interests in Middle Eastern oil.

*III. The Moderate Arab View.*

Although there is some conflict of judgment, the bulk of the evidence before us indicates that the moderate Arab view--as well as the view among our Ambassadors to the Arab world--is that it would be wiser for the Israelis to deal with the present situation than it would be for us.

*IV. The U.S. Interest and Our Task.*

--To open the Gulf of Aqaba to at least oil for Israel--which has become the test of who wins this trial of will and nerve--without war if possible.

--To do so in ways which maximize the chance of long-run peace in the area, including movement towards acceptance of Israel as part of the Middle East.

--In any case, to honor all commitments made in 1957--even, if, in the end, an Arab-Israeli war comes about; that is, our commitment to put through a U.S. flagship; to assert the right of free passage for others; and to regard Israeli counteraction to a UAR attempt to close Aqaba by armed force as involving for Israel legitimate rights of self-defense under the UN Charter.

--To act, in general, in such a way as to unify the political base in the U.S. around our Middle East policy so that we do not weaken the political foundations for our further conduct of the war in Viet Nam.

*V. A Possible Scenario.*

## *Appendix B: Arab-Israeli Crisis and War, 1967*

Here are the main elements in a scenario and their sequence--required to achieve these objectives.

--First, we must urgently make it clear to Nasser--which has not yet been made clear--that we intend to honor our 1957 commitments. His letter to you completely ignores what happened in 1957. He must be reminded that we undertook our commitments in order to get the Israelis off his neck; and it is a matter of honor and continuity of the American word that these commitments be honored. (In this context, a statement by General Eisenhower, and perhaps even a special visit to Cairo by Cabot Lodge--who was personally and directly involved in those events--may be important, as well as our conversations with Mohieddin and your reply to Nasser's letter.)/2/

/2/See footnote 2, Document 148.

In making this point clear, we must also present to him a willingness to move forward with other critical issues in the area where progress is required, if, indeed, the region is to settle down and move towards peace and stability, including: the placement of UN observers on both sides of the borders; Arab refugees; regional economic development; water; and the damping down of the arms race. There is considerable legitimate argument as to whether Nasser is now postured as a Hitler, determined at all costs to exploit temporary Arab unity to crush Israel once and for all, or whether he is a shrewd operator, working off a weak base, willing to settle for as much as he can get from this crisis. If the latter is the case, a package deal of this kind is the best way to smoke him out. If he wants war, the Israelis and we will be in much better shape if we have laid the deal before the world.

--In any case, so far as U.S. public opinion is concerned, opinion in the Middle East, and opinion in the world, we must quickly produce a posture in which the hard-core issue of oil through Aqaba is diluted by the evocation of a larger, more attractive, and more basic objective; namely, to begin to transform the Middle East from its present dangerous, unstable situation into one in which there is the possibility, at least, of movement forwards toward cooperation, development and acceptance of Israel as part of the region.

--By the time we have transmitted this offer to Nasser, we would also have been able to take stock of the response to the declaration of innocent passage through Aqaba and have some feel for how many countries are willing to escort vessels going through the Gulf to Eilat. The stage would then be set for going to Congress and asking for a resolution. (About, say, Thursday of the coming week.)

## Deadly Dogma:
## How Neoconservatives Broke the Law to Deceive America

--The resolution for which we would ask in this scenario would have these characteristics: It would recall and state the three 1957 commitments; it would empower us to use force, if necessary, to support the transit of Aqaba by U.S. flagships and those of other nations, except Israel; it would recognize the government of Israel's expressed desire that it handle the question of its own flagships with its own force; but it would recognize that if the transit of such ships was met by armed force, the Israelis had the right of self-defense. The resolution would call for all parties to permit transit of the Gulf on the basis of the situation between 1957 and the present crisis; and it would appeal for movement forward with respect to peace in the area, including action on UN observers, refugees, development, the regional arms race, etc.

--Behind the scene we would be working for an Aqaba formula in which the oil flow would continue to Eilat; the Israelis would maintain their claim to put flagships through, but not exercise it; the UAR would ignore the fishing trawlers that go in and out of the Gulf; the International Court of Justice would take over the legal controversy involved; the forces in Sinai would demobilize; and, in this interval, we would try to get the Middle East and the world community to go to work on UN observers; refugees; development; etc. (With that kind of resolution and an explicit understanding that we would recognize Israeli rights of self-defense if their vessels were stopped by armed force, it might be possible to hold the Israelis for another week; that is, from Sunday, June 11 (roughly their present D-day) to the 18th of June. In that interval we would have to do two things: bring maximum pressure to bear to get a diplomatic settlement, including maximum pressure on Moscow; and organize a forcing of the blockade in terms of something like the following sequence, designed to fulfill the three U.S. commitments.

--A U.S. vessel goes through with escort, bearing a civilian non-strategic cargo; although it might contain oil. On present evidence, that vessel would not be fired on, although if it contained oil it might be contested.

--A non-U.S. flagship (either Israeli-owned or not) would go through with a civil cargo, backed by whomever the naval powers turn out to be;

--Then, finally, an Israeli vessel would go through and the issue would be put squarely to Nasser to whether he would fire upon it, our having made it clear that we regard Israeli rights of self-defense as legitimate, if armed force were used to stop it; but the background to such Israelis forcing action would be a known formula that if oil were permitted to flow to Eilat, the Israelis were willing to have the whole matter put to the International Court of Justice.

*VI. There are several gut questions unresolved in this proposed scenario, among them these:*

*--Timing and the Israeli tactical military situation.* As we now know, they would prefer to go directly to the test of the Israeli flag, and, in effect, have us stand down on our other commitments, except, of course, our commitment to regard their case as legitimate. Another reason they may wish this to have some element of control over the time which Nasser faces this showdown. If the objective of the exercise is a situation where we achieve oil to Eilat without a war, marching down quite openly to the sequence described above, is a superior scenario. It would also relieve us of a most dangerous problem; namely, of our knowing Israeli plans but holding them secret as did the British and French at the time of Suez, with all the consequent ugly debate and controversy which continued down to the present day. Our interest, and, in fact, the Israeli interest is to do this job like the sheriff in "High Noon", rather than through tactical surprise and quiet secret understandings between Tel Aviv and Washington.

*--If we regard the transit of oil as the gut issue here, when should oil be brought in and under whose flag?* On this I have no firm judgment but suspect the best auspices would be the most natural situation: a foreign flag backed by the escorting party. But there is some virtue in our taking oil in--preferably not Iranian oil with the U.S. flag flying.

*--What, precisely, is the formula for Aqaba that Israel would accept?* Is it prepared to accept a situation where oil goes through while the issue is taken to the International Court of Justice; trawlers go through with Israeli flag de facto; but, while reserving their legal rights to put Israeli flags through, they do not test that right until the International Court of Justice rules? My inclination would be to use maximum leverage with the Israelis to accept such a deal if Nasser accepts it, demobilizes his forces in Sinai, and accepts the agenda of UN observers; some progress on refugees; development; arms race talks; etc.

*VII. USSR.*

In the end, whether the outcome is an Arab-Israeli war or a successful transit of the crisis depends a good deal on the USSR. If we move in the way I have indicated, I am moderately optimistic that they will, in the clutch, throw considerable weight on Cairo to accept a pragmatic deal for the following reasons:

--They would not like to see U.S. and other naval powers actually exercised to force the Gulf of Aqaba for non-Israeli ships.

--I believe they honestly fear an Arab-Israeli war because they still believe that the Israelis will win it. If they win it after more than 10 years of pouring Soviet arms into the Middle East, the whole Soviet arms game will be profoundly degraded. It has already been substantially degraded by the outcome in Indonesia. If their military men calculate, like ours, that, at considerable cost in blood, the Israelis could now beat the Arabs armed with Soviet MIG-21s and Soviet tanks, they would do a good deal to avoid that demonstration. On reflection, I suspect this factor has played a big role in their anxiety about the Israelis launching an attack.

--Finally, they have carefully not committed themselves on the question of Aqaba and left it open for them, in the end, to play a kind of Tashkent role./3/

/3/Reference is to the Soviet role in bringing about the Tashkent Communiqu□ of January 10, 1966, in which India and Pakistan agreed to withdraw their forces to positions held before the 1965 fighting in Kashmir.

--Therefore, if we move down this track and assert through the Congress our willingness to back our play on all three 1957 commitments, my hunch is that they will move rather fast to come up with their own kind of formula to avoid the war and try to portray their role as frustrating the designs of American imperialists and Israeli lackeys. If it all ends up with oil going to Eilat, the forces demobilized, UN observers, talk about refugees, development, etc., that would be quite okay with us.

WWR

## 145. Telegram From the Embassy in the United Arab Republic to the Department of State/1/

Cairo, June 4, 1967, 1925Z.

/1/Source: National Archives and Records Administration, RG 59, Central Files 1967-69, POL ARAB-ISR. Secret; Flash; Nodis. Received at 3:44 p.m. Rostow sent a copy to the President at 5:15 p.m. (Johnson Library, National Security File, Country File, Middle East Crisis, Vol. III)

8384. Ref: Cairo 8471./2/

/2/Nolte reported in telegram 8471 from Cairo, June 4, that the Embassy had informed Riad of the contents of telegram 207861 to Cairo (see footnote 2, Document 134), and that he planned to take up the subject of Mohieddin's visit with Nasser when presenting his credentials on June 5. (National Archives and Records Administration, RG 59, Central Files 1967-69, POL ARAB-ISR) Rusk responded to the latter point in telegram 207994, June 4, which reads in part: "The great value of Mohieddin's visit is opportunity for private discussions. The less said about it the better." (Johnson Library, National Security File, Country File, Middle East Crisis, Anderson Cables)

1. Charg☐ Nes has just been called separately by Ashraf Ghorbal of Foreign Office and Mustapha Aziz of Presidency and told that Zakariya Mohieddin plans leave for Washington Wednesday June 7.

2. Party will include Mustapha Aziz, perhaps Deputy Prime Minister Fawzi and others. Details of party and travel plans will be given us tomorrow. Charg☐ has offered all assistance. Ghorbal leaving tomorrow as advance party, with ETA Washington Tuesday.

3. Indications are that Mohieddin will wish discuss totality Palestine problem, resolution of which would permit regulation Tiran Straits issue. More on this later as may be possible following any discussions we may be able have with delegation members prior their departure.

Nolte

**146. Telegram From the Department of State to the Embassy in the United Kingdom/1/**

Washington, June 4, 1967, 9:54 p.m.

/1/Source: National Archives and Records Administration, RG 59, Central Files 1967-69, POL ARAB-ISR. Secret; Exdis. Drafted by Eugene Rostow's Special Assistant Alan R. Novak, and approved by Rostow.

208026. Middle East Crisis.

Ambassador Dean called on Under Secretary Rostow this afternoon at Rostow's request.

1. Rostow assured Ambassador British Government notified immediately if we had indication Israeli decision to force Strait alone. Dean stressed UK would not support such unilateral Israeli action. UK recognized that under international law and 1957 arrangements, US/UK position was that Israel justified in striking back if Israeli ship turned back by armed force. UK position, however, was that unescorted probe was invitation to Egyptians to fire. UK support for escorted probe based on judgment that UAR would not fire.

2. Rostow reported clearance obtained today on constituting international naval force. Instructions going out today/2/ and Ambassador Harriman would make some special approaches coming week. Entire effort would be coordinated with UK Ambassadors.

/2/A memorandum of June 9 from Deane R. Hinton of EUR/RPE to Walsh states that at the time of the outbreak of hostilities, an instruction to the Embassies in a number of countries was awaiting approval by the Secretary. Hinton's memorandum is filed with what he describes as a draft history of the MADEC operation. The attachment is headed: "The Middle East Crisis: Activities of the Task Force Subcommittee on the Maritime Declaration." It includes a brief chronology and 24 attachments. (Ibid., Middle East Crisis Files, E. 5190, Box 14, History of MADEC) Other files on the Maritime Declaration effort are ibid., Box 13.

3. Some countries had minor problems of wording in maritime declaration. Dean and Rostow agreed that to save time, such countries might make slight alterations in the wording of the declaration and then file separate declarations under common covering letter to the UN. (Further instructions on this are to follow.)

4. Joint naval planning with UK EmbOff starts Tuesday,/3/ with London group Wednesday.

/3/June 6.

Rusk

**147. Memorandum From the Contingency Work Group on Military Planning to the Middle East Control Group/1/**

Washington, June 4, 1967.

# Appendix B: Arab-Israeli Crisis and War, 1967

/1/Source: Washington National Records Center, OSD Files: FRC 330 72 A 2468, Middle East 381.3. Secret. Sent to Secretary of Defense McNamara with a covering memorandum of June 4 from Hoopes that states the Control Group was to consider it "preliminary" that evening. A stamped notation on the memorandum indicates that McNamara saw it on June 5. A copy of a JCS memorandum for McNamara on "Military Actions--Straits of Tiran," JCSM-310-67, June 2, is attached. It discussed possible military forces that might be used and steps that might be taken in case a decision were made to test the UAR blockade, with the assumption that more time was available than had been assumed in JCSM-301-67, May 27, which had considered only actions that could be taken within approximately 1 week. (See footnote 2, Document 91.)

SUBJECT
Measures to Test or Force the Tiran Blockade

This paper explores the prospects for unescorted and escorted tests of the UAR blockade of the Strait of Tiran. We face a choice between two basic strategies: (1) a series of tests backed by a naval escort force representing the maritime nations, with the intent to assert free passage by force if necessary; or (2) a test or series of tests sponsored by Israel, with the understanding that if passage is refused Israeli military action (limited or broad-scale) would follow.

During the past week we have also discussed the utility of unescorted tests designed merely to define the limits of the blockade and to build a case for international political or juridical action to relieve it. Under that concept, there is no necessary relationship between the tests and the ultimate decision to organize and use an escort force. This approach seems less relevant now, in view of our greater knowledge concerning the UAR blockade and of the pressures of time.

*The Feasibility of Arranging Tests*

Under the first choice above, the requirement is two-fold: to assemble test ships of appropriate registries and in sufficient numbers, and to assemble an international naval escort force representing the maritime nations. The neuralgic points of the blockade are (a) oil, (b) Israeli flag vessels, and (c) possibly Israeli-owned vessels.

[Omitted here is discussion of the problems of assembling test ships and an international escort force, possibilities of unescorted passage by U.S. flag or non-U.S. flag tankers and possible consequences, consequences of a test by an unescorted Israeli vessel, the possibility of an escorted probe by a non-Israeli vessel and its possible consequences, and the possibility of an Israeli-sponsored test of the blockade.]

*Conclusions*

1. It is important to understand that we face a clear choice between basic, mutually exclusive strategies for testing the blockade. The deliberate attempt to combine them would almost surely produce the worst possible consequences for US interests, as would their intermingling by inadvertence or calculated Israeli action.

2. A US decision to assume responsibility for testing the blockade leads inevitably to the requirement for a naval escort force; and given the probability that the UAR will turn back unescorted tankers (including those of US registry), the organization of a naval escort force will lead almost certainly to its use.

3. The mere organization of such an escort force would be construed as a hostile act by the UAR, and would produce serious political and economic retaliation against US interests throughout the Arab world. On balance, however, these may be manageable if the force is not actually used.

4. The actual use [of] the escort force would produce graver political and economic consequences for US interests (even if the UAR did not resist militarily and the USSR exercised great caution). These would likely include seizure or nationalization of oil companies, closure of the Suez Canal to nations participating in the force, cut-off of oil pipelines to the Mediterranean, and UN action that might either charge the US with "aggression" or place further US actions to run the blockade in violation of the UN. In addition, mob violence against US life and property in the Middle East would be probable.

5. A brief, inconclusive military engagement between the UAR and the escort force would intensify, but not materially alter, the consequences set out in paragraph 4.

6. A serious UAR military effort to prevent escorted passage would project the US into a state of war with the UAR, with no logical or mutually acceptable break-off point. The fact of US belligerency would gravely diminish the possibilities of Soviet restraint in its support of the Arabs, or of joint US-Soviet efforts to limit and terminate hostilities. Such a situation could be quickly escalated and complicated by a major Israeli attack on the Arabs, or a major Arab attack on Israel.

Either contingency would be probable if serious fighting between the escort force and the UAR developed in the Strait of Tiran.

7. Under the best possible circumstances (i.e., broad and vigorous adherence to the maritime declaration and a truly international escort force), it might be possible to separate the issue of free passage from the basic Arab-Israeli conflict. But given the present facts (i.e., a fairly narrow, lukewarm support for the declaration and a marked lack of enthusiasm for the escort force) such a separation is illusory. Thus if the escort force were used, UAR and Soviet propaganda would succeed in linking the two issues, and in branding the US as the enemy of the Arabs.

8. The strategy involving US-sponsored tests plus an escort force cannot therefore serve US interests in existing circumstances. At best, its pursuit would further polarize Middle East politics, pitting the US and Israel against the USSR and all the Arab states, with the gravest political and economic damage to US and West European interests; at worst, it would embroil the US in a direct war with Nasser and the Arabs, with the serious danger of rapid escalation to military confrontation with the USSR.

9. The alternative basic strategy of an Israeli-sponsored probe would almost surely lead to Arab-Israeli hostilities. An unescorted vessel (either Israeli flag or Israeli owned) would almost certainly be turned back. If it resisted, it would be fired on; Israel would then retaliate, leading to widespread hostilities.

10. A probe sponsored by Israel would have one cardinal advantage. It is that, in the event of hostilities, the US and the USSR would not be directly engaged and would share a mutual interest in limiting the conflict at some point. When this point became manifest, it is reasonable to hope that they would find it possible to cooperate in bringing an end to hostilities and in providing support, both in and outside the UN, for a peaceful settlement. Thus, on the judgment that some bloodletting is an unavoidable precondition to any new political settlement, the alternative basic strategy has the greater merit, in terms of protecting US vital interests and preserving the fabric of world peace.

11. If the US were a belligerent, the chances for limiting and ending hostilities would be infinitely worsened, in part because the UN would be rendered impotent (as in the case of Vietnam) by a fundamental split between the two superpowers.

12. The choice between these two basic strategies for testing the blockade is a cruel one. Pursuit of the first strategy will lead almost inevitably to a total polarization of Middle East politics with the gravest damage to US political and economic interests in that area; and the risks are substantial that it would also lead to war in which the US would be embroiled. Pursuit of the alternative basic strategy will lead almost inevitably to widespread Arab-Israeli hostilities, in which, however, the US could probably avoid direct involvement.

13. The cruelty of the choice impels one to turn to more intensive work on the elements of a third possibility--a compromise political settlement, a course which is beyond the scope of this paper. It is vitally important to recognize that the chances of reaching a political settlement based on less than the maximum demands of Israel and the UAR on the blockade issue (e.g., a settlement based on tacit acceptance by the UAR of the passage of non-Israeli tankers, and tacit agreement by Israel not to demand more) would be sharply reduced, if not eliminated, by a prior resort to either testing strategy. This conclusion points to the critical importance of (a) avoiding actions which would now commit us to the first basic strategy, and of (b) persuading Israel to forego action in the Gulf until all reasonable efforts toward a peaceful effort have failed.

Townsend Hoopes/2/
*Chairman*

/2/Printed from a copy that bears this typed signature.

**148. Minutes of the Ninth Meeting of the Middle East Control Group/1/**

Washington, June 4, 1967, 11 a.m.

/1/Source: National Archives and Records Administration, RG 59, Office of the Executive Secretariat, Middle East Crisis Files, 1967, Entry 5190, Box 17, Minutes/Decisions of the Control Group, Folder 1. Secret; Nodis. No drafter or participants are on the source text.

The Control Group Meeting, which began in the morning and continued into the evening, concluded with a meeting with Secretary Rusk, Secretary McNamara, NSC Special Representative Walt Rostow, and Ambassador Thompson. The main element throughout the day was preparation for the visit of the UAR Vice President Mohieddin.

## *Appendix B: Arab-Israeli Crisis and War, 1967*

The Group began its discussions with a review of the actions taken since the beginning of the crisis. These included:

1. Presidential messages to the Heads of State of the countries of the area, urging restraint.

2. Continuing efforts in various ways to hold the Israeli "tiger".

3. Structural organization for the crisis, including the establishment of the Task Force and the Control Group. The latter knitted together State, DOD, the White House, CIA and Treasury. Planning had been wide-ranging and in depth.

4. Direct discussions had been held in Washington with UK Minister of State George Thomson and his delegation. There had been a meeting of minds on an assessment of the gravity of the situation. In addition, on an ad referendum working level basis, there had been agreement on a course of action involving (a) intensive use of UN facilities in an effort to de-fuse the situation; (b) the preparation of a Maritime Declaration which would express the views and positions of the Maritime Powers on the Gulf of Aqaba and would win maximum international support; (c) bringing into being a multination naval force which, if all political means failed, could provide escorts for passage through the Straits of Tiran.

5. Israeli Foreign Minister Eban had visited Washington and had discussed the crisis with the President, Secretary Rusk, Secretary McNamara, and Members of the Control Group. He explained that the Israeli Cabinet confronted by the alternatives of war or surrender, had chosen the former, only to be restrained by the intervention, under instructions, of Ambassador Barbour, who had presented a "third alternative". A determined effort had been made to dissuade the Israeli Government from resorting to military action. This included an exposition of the "third alternative" of diplomatic activity in the UN and elsewhere, the Maritime Declaration, and the assembly of a Naval Force for possible use in the Red Sea and the Gulf of Aqaba.

6. There had been continuing recourse to the Security Council.

7. There had been extensive diplomatic contacts in Washington and in pertinent capitals around the world.

8. There had been extensive consultations with Congress in respect to the developing situation.

# Deadly Dogma:
## How Neoconservatives Broke the Law to Deceive America

9. Private emissaries had been sent to the area:

a. Charles Yost had been sent to Cairo to help Ambassador Nolte, who had not been able to present his credentials, and to take soundings with members of the UAR Government;

b. Robert Anderson, former Secretary of Treasury, had been in direct contact with President Nasser and had set the stage for the visit of Vice President Zakaria Mohieddin. Nasser had expressed in a letter to the President his willingness to send Mohieddin to Washington or to receive Vice President Humphrey in Cairo.

c. Governor Harriman had been in direct contact with the Shah of Iran.

d. Arrangements had been made for Presidential Counsel Harry McPherson to visit Tel Aviv.

While the original objective of the Control Group had been--starkly stated--to prevent the Israelis from striking the forces closing around them, its objectives had now broadened to include: (1) avoiding either an Israeli-UAR war or a clash between the Maritime Powers and the Arabs, and (2) developing the basic ingredients of an enduring peace in the Middle East.

The immediate tasks before the Group were to complete the staff work for the Mohieddin visit. This was to include the preparation of (1) a viable negotiating position with the UAR; (2) the formulation of assurances acceptable to Israel; and (3) the development of a scenario for use if the negotiations with the UAR should fail. It was noted that the difficulties of these tasks were compounded by (1) the obscurity of UAR objectives, (2) the heavy engagement of Nasser's prestige and the indication that he was striving for a major political victory; (3) the military confrontation of highly mobilized Arab and Israeli forces; and (4) the limited degree of our control over Israel.

As the day wore on, it became evident that Mohieddin would not arrive before the evening of June 7 and talks would not begin before the following day. Furthermore, press tickers from Cairo indicated that the UARG intended to give heavy propaganda treatment to the visit. In view of the manifest dangers that an incident could at any time lead to a clash between the heavily mobilized Arab and Israeli forces, cables were sent to Cairo urging Mohieddin to expedite his arrival, and emphasizing that minimum publicity was desirable. Although the Secretary had informed the Israeli Ambassador of the visit, it was evident that a heavy propaganda play by Cairo would create difficulty for the Israelis. It would also intensify the inherent problem of security. It was agreed that the physical arrangements for the visit, including security, would be delegated to Idar Rimestad, Deputy Under Secretary for Administration, and James Symington, Chief of Protocol. A maximum security effort would be made.

During the course of the day, the Group considered three documents related to the Mohieddin visit: (a) a memorandum to the President; (b) a draft letter to Nasser;/2/ and (c) a draft letter to Kosygin. These were extensively revised prior to the early evening discussion with the two Secretaries and Walt Rostow. While there was full agreement that a basic memorandum had to be prepared promptly for the President's use in the Mohieddin talks, there were differences of views about the desirability of sending messages to either Kosygin or Nasser before the talks began. Following a thorough review of the advantages and disadvantages, the Secretary decided that (1) the Memorandum for the President, with certain revisions, should be transmitted to the White House on June 5; (2) he would revise the draft letter to Nasser, with certain "Levantine touches" with the thought that it might constitute a basic talking paper and be presented to Mohieddin when he met the President; (3) the letter to Kosygin should not be sent at this time but a revised letter might be sent after the meeting with Mohieddin.

/2/The June 4 draft letter to Nasser is filed with two draft memoranda to the President, both undated. The draft letter bears the handwritten note: "Sec was changing this when time ran out." (Ibid., Central Files 1967-69, POL 15-1 US/Johnson)

The draft Memorandum for the President contained the following elements of assessment: (1) time is running out and the Israelis may not stand for more than another week; (2) the rumors of a naval escort plan may be having some effect on Nasser, but the value of the idea as a diplomatic pressure is lessened by the doubts that are being spread by the Soviets and others that we are really serious in considering the naval-escort plan as a genuine alternative; (3) our main effort should be concentrated on Nasser and the Soviets. We should be firm on the issue of the Strait, while indicating the possibilities of a broad and constructive settlement at a later stage for the whole region. We should ascertain what is "under the rug". Do they want war or not? (4) Nasser should be made aware that if he actually uses force to close the Strait of Tiran, and the Israelis have recourse to Article 51, they will be doing so pursuant to the terms of a contract President Eisenhower brought about for the benefit of the Israelis and the Egyptians in 1957; (5) we should not try to negotiate with the Egyptians for the Israelis; (6) rather than agree to the exclusion from the Gulf of Israeli flag ships, the Israelis would fight; (7) in view of the possibility that we may have to face the Evron scenario (putting an

Israeli flag ship through the Straits and utilizing armed force under Article 51 if it were attacked) within a few days, it is highly important to make the most strenuous possible diplomatic effort now; (8) the purpose of the proposed letter to Nasser is to get Nasser to stop, look and listen; (9) either an Arab-Israeli war, or the situation that would develop if we, the British, Australians and Dutch forced the Straits, would have great potentialities for hurting our long-term interests in the area, and in the Moslem world; (10) our best option if we can get it within a few days, is to avoid both alternatives without giving Nasser a complete political victory; (11) a maximum political effort is required to restore things as thy were in the Gulf, until either the World Court or a political agreement can settle the problem.

# Appendix C: The Clean Break Plan

## A Clean Break: A New Strategy for Securing the Realm

Following is a report prepared by The Institute for Advanced Strategic and Political Studies' "Study Group on a New Israeli Strategy Toward 2000." The main substantive ideas in this paper emerge from a discussion in which prominent opinion makers, including Richard Perle, James Colbert, Charles Fairbanks, Jr., Douglas Feith, Robert Loewenberg, David Wurmser, and Meyrav Wurmser participated. The report, entitled "A Clean Break: A New Strategy for Securing the Realm," is the framework for a series of follow-up reports on strategy.

Israel has a large problem. Labor Zionism, which for 70 years has dominated the Zionist movement, has generated a stalled and shackled economy. Efforts to salvage Israel's socialist institutions—which include pursuing supranational over national sovereignty and pursuing a peace process that embraces the slogan, "New Middle East"—undermine the legitimacy of the nation and lead Israel into strategic paralysis and the previous government's "peace process." That peace process obscured the evidence of eroding national critical mass— including a palpable sense of national exhaustion—and forfeited strategic initiative. The loss of national critical mass was illustrated best by Israel's efforts to draw in the United States to sell unpopular policies domestically, to agree to negotiate sovereignty over its capital, and to respond with resignation to a spate of terror so intense and tragic that it deterred Israelis from engaging in normal daily functions, such as commuting to work in buses.

Benjamin Netanyahu's government comes in with a new set of ideas. While there are those who will counsel continuity, Israel has the opportunity to make a clean break; it can forge a peace process and strategy based on an entirely new intellectual foundation, one that restores strategic initiative and provides the nation the room to engage every possible energy on rebuilding Zionism, the starting point of which must be economic reform. To secure the nation's streets and borders in the immediate future, Israel can:

* Work closely with Turkey and Jordan to contain, destabilize, and roll-back some of its most dangerous threats. This implies clean break from the slogan, "comprehensive peace" to a traditional concept of strategy based on balance of power.

* Change the nature of its relations with the Palestinians, including upholding the right of hot pursuit for self defense into all Palestinian areas and nurturing alternatives to Arafat's exclusive grip on Palestinian society.

* Forge a new basis for relations with the United States— stressing self-reliance, maturity, strategic cooperation on areas of mutual concern, and furthering values inherent to the West. This can only be done if Israel takes serious steps to terminate aid, which prevents economic reform.

This report is written with key passages of a possible speech marked TEXT, that highlight the clean break which the new government has an opportunity to make. The body of the report is the commentary explaining the purpose and laying out the strategic context of the passages.

<u>A New Approach to Peace</u>

Early adoption of a bold, new perspective on peace and security is imperative for the new prime minister. While the previous government, and many abroad, may emphasize "land for peace"— which placed Israel in the position of cultural, economic, political, diplomatic, and military retreat — the new government can promote Western values and traditions. Such an approach, which will be well received in the United

States, includes "peace for peace," "peace through strength" and self reliance: the balance of power.

A new strategy to seize the initiative can be introduced:

TEXT:

We have for four years pursued peace based on a New Middle East. We in Israel cannot play innocents abroad in a world that is not innocent. Peace depends on the character and behavior of our foes. We live in a dangerous neighborhood, with fragile states and bitter rivalries. Displaying moral ambivalence between the effort to build a Jewish state and the desire to annihilate it by trading "land for peace" will not secure "peace now." Our claim to the land —to which we have clung for hope for 2000 years--is legitimate and noble. It is not within our own power, no matter how much we concede, to make peace unilaterally. Only the unconditional acceptance by Arabs of our rights, especially in their territorial dimension, "peace for peace," is a solid basis for the future.

Israel's quest for peace emerges from, and does not replace, the pursuit of its ideals. The Jewish people's hunger for human rights — burned into their identity by a 2000-year old dream to live free in their own land — informs the concept of peace and reflects continuity of values with Western and Jewish tradition. Israel can now embrace negotiations, but as means, not ends, to pursue those ideals and demonstrate national steadfastness. It can challenge police states; enforce compliance of agreements; and insist on minimal standards of accountability.

Securing the Northern Border

Syria challenges Israel on Lebanese soil. An effective approach, and one with which American can sympathize, would be if Israel seized the strategic initiative along its northern borders by engaging Hizballah, Syria, and Iran, as the principal agents of aggression in Lebanon, including by:

\*   striking Syria's drug-money and counterfeiting infrastructure in Lebanon, all of which focuses on Razi Qanan.

* paralleling Syria's behavior by establishing the precedent that Syrian territory is not immune to attacks emanating from Lebanon by Israeli proxy forces.

* striking Syrian military targets in Lebanon, and should that prove insufficient, striking at select targets in Syria proper.

Israel also can take this opportunity to remind the world of the nature of the Syrian regime. Syria repeatedly breaks its word. It violated numerous agreements with the Turks, and has betrayed the United States by continuing to occupy Lebanon in violation of the Taef agreement in 1989. Instead, Syria staged a sham election, installed a quisling regime, and forced Lebanon to sign a "Brotherhood Agreement" in 1991, that terminated Lebanese sovereignty. And Syria has begun colonizing Lebanon with hundreds of thousands of Syrians, while killing tens of thousands of its own citizens at a time, as it did in only three days in 1983 in Hama.

Under Syrian tutelage, the Lebanese drug trade, for which local Syrian military officers receive protection payments, flourishes. Syria's regime supports the terrorist groups operationally and financially in Lebanon and on its soil. Indeed, the Syrian-controlled Bekaa Valley in Lebanon has become for terror what the Silicon Valley has become for computers. The Bekaa Valley has become one of the main distribution sources, if not production points, of the "supernote" — counterfeit US currency so well done that it is impossible to detect.

Text:

Negotiations with repressive regimes like Syria's require cautious realism. One cannot sensibly assume the other side's good faith. It is dangerous for Israel to deal naively with a regime murderous of its own people, openly aggressive toward its neighbors, criminally involved with international drug traffickers and counterfeiters, and supportive of the most deadly terrorist organizations.

## *Appendix C: A Clean Break*

Given the nature of the regime in Damascus, it is both natural and moral that Israel abandon the slogan "comprehensive peace" and move to contain Syria, drawing attention to its weapons of mass destruction program, and rejecting "land for peace" deals on the Golan Heights.

Moving to a Traditional Balance of Power Strategy

TEXT:

We must distinguish soberly and clearly friend from foe. We must make sure that our friends across the Middle East never doubt the solidity or value of our friendship.

Israel can shape its strategic environment, in cooperation with Turkey and Jordan, by weakening, containing, and even rolling back Syria. This effort can focus on removing Saddam Hussein from power in Iraq — an important Israeli strategic objective in its own right — as a means of foiling Syria's regional ambitions. Jordan has challenged Syria's regional ambitions recently by suggesting the restoration of the Hashemites in Iraq. This has triggered a Jordanian-Syrian rivalry to which Asad has responded by stepping up efforts to destabilize the Hashemite Kingdom, including using infiltrations. Syria recently signaled that it and Iran might prefer a weak, but barely surviving Saddam, if only to undermine and humiliate Jordan in its efforts to remove Saddam.

But Syria enters this conflict with potential weaknesses: Damascus is too preoccupied with dealing with the threatened new regional equation to permit distractions of the Lebanese flank. And Damascus fears that the 'natural axis' with Israel on one side, central Iraq and Turkey on the other, and Jordan, in the center would squeeze and detach Syria from the Saudi Peninsula. For Syria, this could be the prelude to a redrawing of the map of the Middle East which would threaten Syria's territorial integrity.

Since Iraq's future could affect the strategic balance in the Middle East profoundly, it would be understandable that Israel has an interest in supporting the Hashemites in their efforts to redefine Iraq, including such measures as: visiting Jordan as the first official state visit, even before a visit to the United States, of the new Netanyahu government; supporting King Hussein by providing him with some tangible security measures to protect his regime against Syrian subversion; encouraging — through influence in the U.S. business community — investment in Jordan to structurally shift Jordan's economy away from dependence on Iraq; and diverting Syria's attention by using Lebanese opposition elements to destabilize Syrian control of Lebanon.

Most important, it is understandable that Israel has an interest supporting diplomatically, militarily and operationally Turkey's and Jordan's actions against Syria, such as securing tribal alliances with Arab tribes that cross into Syrian territory and are hostile to the Syrian ruling elite.

King Hussein may have ideas for Israel in bringing its Lebanon problem under control. The predominantly Shia population of southern Lebanon has been tied for centuries to the Shia leadership in Najf, Iraq rather than Iran. Were the Hashemites to control Iraq, they could use their influence over Najf to help Israel wean the south Lebanese Shia away from Hizballah, Iran, and Syria. Shia retain strong ties to the Hashemites: the Shia venerate foremost the Prophet's family, the direct descendants of which — and in whose veins the blood of the Prophet flows — is King Hussein.

## Changing the Nature of Relations with the Palestinians

Israel has a chance to forge a new relationship between itself and the Palestinians. First and foremost, Israel's efforts to secure its streets may require hot pursuit into Palestinian-controlled areas, a justifiable practice with which Americans can sympathize.

A key element of peace is compliance with agreements already signed. Therefore, Israel has the right to insist on compliance, including closing Orient House and disbanding

Jibril Rujoub's operatives in Jerusalem. Moreover, Israel and the United States can establish a Joint Compliance Monitoring Committee to study periodically whether the PLO meets minimum standards of compliance, authority and responsibility, human rights, and judicial and fiduciary accountability.

TEXT:

We believe that the Palestinian Authority must be held to the same minimal standards of accountability as other recipients of U.S. foreign aid. A firm peace cannot tolerate repression and injustice. A regime that cannot fulfill the most rudimentary obligations to its own people cannot be counted upon to fulfill its obligations to its neighbors.

Israel has no obligations under the Oslo agreements if the PLO does not fulfill its obligations. If the PLO cannot comply with these minimal standards, then it can be neither a hope for the future nor a proper interlocutor for present. To prepare for this, Israel may want to cultivate alternatives to Arafat's base of power. Jordan has ideas on this.

To emphasize the point that Israel regards the actions of the PLO problematic, but not the Arab people, Israel might want to consider making a special effort to reward friends and advance human rights among Arabs. Many Arabs are willing to work with Israel; identifying and helping them are important. Israel may also find that many of her neighbors, such as Jordan, have problems with Arafat and may want to cooperate. Israel may also want to better integrate its own Arabs.

Forging A New U.S.-Israeli Relationship

In recent years, Israel invited active U.S. intervention in Israel's domestic and foreign policy for two reasons: to overcome domestic opposition to "land for peace" concessions the Israeli public could not digest, and to lure Arabs —

through money, forgiveness of past sins, and access to U.S. weapons — to negotiate. This strategy, which required funneling American money to repressive and aggressive regimes, was risky, expensive, and very costly for both the U.S. and Israel, and placed the United States in roles is should neither have nor want.

Israel can make a clean break from the past and establish a new vision for the U.S.-Israeli partnership based on self-reliance, maturity and mutuality — not one focused narrowly on territorial disputes. Israel's new strategy — based on a shared philosophy of peace through strength — reflects continuity with Western values by stressing that Israel is self-reliant, does not need U.S. troops in any capacity to defend it, including on the Golan Heights, and can manage its own affairs. Such self-reliance will grant Israel greater freedom of action and remove a significant lever of pressure used against it in the past.

To reinforce this point, the Prime Minister can use his forthcoming visit to announce that Israel is now mature enough to cut itself free immediately from at least U.S. economic aid and loan guarantees at least, which prevent economic reform. [Military aid is separated for the moment until adequate arrangements can be made to ensure that Israel will not encounter supply problems in the means to defend itself]. As outlined in another Institute report, Israel can become self-reliant only by, in a bold stroke rather than in increments, liberalizing its economy, cutting taxes, relegislating a free-processing zone, and selling-off public lands and enterprises — moves which will electrify and find support from a broad bipartisan spectrum of key pro-Israeli Congressional leaders, including Speaker of the House, Newt Gingrich.

Israel can under these conditions better cooperate with the U.S. to counter real threats to the region and the West's security. Mr. Netanyahu can highlight his desire to cooperate more closely with the United States on anti-missile defense in order to remove the threat of blackmail which even a weak and distant army can pose to either state. Not only would such cooperation on missile defense counter a tangible physical threat to Israel's survival, but it would broaden Israel's base of support among many in the United States Congress who may know little about Israel, but care very much about missile defense. Such broad support could be helpful in the effort to move the U.S. embassy in Israel to Jerusalem.

To anticipate U.S. reactions and plan ways to manage and constrain those reactions, Prime Minister Netanyahu can formulate the policies and stress themes he favors in language familiar to the Americans by tapping into themes of American administrations during the Cold War which apply well to Israel. If Israel wants to test certain propositions that require a benign American reaction, then the best time to do so is before November, 1996.

Conclusions: Transcending the Arab-Israeli Conflict

TEXT: Israel will not only contain its foes; it will transcend them.

Notable Arab intellectuals have written extensively on their perception of Israel's floundering and loss of national identity. This perception has invited attack, blocked Israel from achieving true peace, and offered hope for those who would destroy Israel. The previous strategy, therefore, was leading the Middle East toward another Arab-Israeli war. Israel's new agenda can signal a clean break by abandoning a policy which assumed exhaustion and allowed strategic retreat by reestablishing the principle of preemption, rather than retaliation alone and by ceasing to absorb blows to the nation without response.

Israel's new strategic agenda can shape the regional environment in ways that grant Israel the room to refocus its energies back to where they are most needed: to rejuvenate its national idea, which can only come through replacing Israel's socialist foundations with a more sound footing; and to overcome its "exhaustion," which threatens the survival of the nation.

## Deadly Dogma:
### How Neoconservatives Broke the Law to Deceive America

Ultimately, Israel can do more than simply manage the Arab-Israeli conflict though war. No amount of weapons or victories will grant Israel the peace its seeks. When Israel is on a sound economic footing, and is free, powerful, and healthy internally, it will no longer simply manage the Arab-Israeli conflict; it will transcend it. As a senior Iraqi opposition leader said recently: "Israel must rejuvenate and revitalize its moral and intellectual leadership. It is an important — if not the most important--element in the history of the Middle East." Israel — proud, wealthy, solid, and strong — would be the basis of a truly new and peaceful Middle East.

Participants in the Study Group on "A New Israeli Strategy Toward 2000:"

Richard Perle, American Enterprise Institute, Study Group Leader

James Colbert, Jewish Institute for National Security Affairs

Charles Fairbanks, Jr., Johns Hopkins University/SAIS

Douglas Feith, Feith and Zell Associates

Robert Loewenberg, President, Institute for Advanced Strategic and Political Studies

Jonathan Torop, The Washington Institute for Near East Policy

David Wurmser, Institute for Advanced Strategic and Political Studies

Meyrav Wurmser, Johns Hopkins University

# Appendix D: Gas Stations in the Sky

Wall Street Journal

Aug 14, 2003

Authors: Thomas Donnelly and Richard Perle

One of the clearest "lessons learned" from Operation Iraqi Freedom is that traditional assumptions about the proper "tooth-to-tail" ratio—that is, the proportion of forces that do the actual fighting to those that support combat operations—need to be rethought. It is likewise clear that this will require changes in the way the Defense Department procures its weaponry.

Operation Iraqi Freedom scored a very large military victory with a very small fighting force, on a vast battlefield measuring tens of thousands of square miles. By any standard, we suffered very few losses and very little attrition along the way, arriving in Baghdad on Day 21 as ready to fight as on D-Day.

Thus, in Iraq, the limits on American military power were defined less by the tooth than by the tail. Consider the air campaign: On an average day, about 1,500 sorties were flown, of which only half were actual strike sorties. More than one-quarter were refueling missions—over 9,000 tanker sorties in total.

Without these tanker aircraft, projecting and sustaining airpower would not be possible. While longer-range bombers and cruise missiles hit some Iraqi targets, the overwhelming majority of the strike sorties were flown by the shorter-range, tactical aircraft that depend on midair refueling.

These swarms of fighter-bombers, along with close air support aircraft, were the key to the flexible, air-ground coordination at the heart of the new American way of war.

Refueling tankers likewise kept open the northern front in Iraq. After Turkey refused to open its borders to a coalition ground force, U.S. commanders had to rely upon a mix of airpower and a small number of Special Forces to turn the tide in the north. Aircraft from the Mediterranean were able to reach into Iraq only because of tankers based in Romania and Bulgaria.

In Afghanistan, too, where the Pentagon relied even more heavily on airpower, our ability to extend operational range with airborne refueling made all the difference. A mission of B-52s flown out of Guam, for instance, required 48 support tankers. Any future operations in northeast Asia—over the Korean Peninsula or the Taiwan Strait—would not be possible without extensive refueling support. In short, U.S. airpower would not be a global force but for the ability to conduct aerial refueling.

Unfortunately, the defense drawdown of the 1990s did real damage to less-glamorous support forces like aerial refueling. The average age of KC-135 tanker aircraft is more than 40 years old—or more than 10 years older than the rest of the Air Force fleet. At any given time, about one-third of the KC-135 fleet is out of service for repairs, and the "E" model spends an average of 400 days in costly depot-level maintenance.

Indeed, tankers risk being the Achilles' heel of American airpower. Just as the requirements for long-range power projection are increasing, the resources to enable them are increasingly insufficient. As outgoing Air Force Secretary James Roche put it: "My fear is that our tanker fleet could be the [lost] horseshoe nail that could cause the horse to tumble, the king to fall, and the kingdom to come apart."

Although the Air Force has devised an innovative proposal to assure an adequate tanker fleet, it has become bogged down in bureaucracy. If ever there were an argument that traditional business practices are ill-suited for defense "transformation," the saga of the tanker-leasing proposal would count as People's Exhibit A.

The problem is this: The Air Force's approved, pre-9/11 procurement program contained no real money to replace aging tankers or—better still—expand the fleet to meet growing requirements. Mr. Roche's clever solution, familiar to every American who has leased his or her automobile rather than purchasing it outright, was to lease 767 tankers as efficient "gas stations in the sky." Even better, the Air Force could acquire the new tankers outright when the term of the lease is complete, or anytime in between.

Perhaps inevitably, this new approach to procurement riled the bureaucracy, with the General Accounting Office—charged to take the narrowest possible analysis—concluding that "the urgency of [tanker] replacement is unclear." After all, until Sept. 11, the Air Force never mentioned the need for tankers in its annual "unfunded requirements" list.

It takes a special government green-eyeshade mentality to miss the urgency of the tanker requirement. Government calculations almost always are based on straight-line projections that the future will be just like the past; but big events like the war on terrorism simply cannot be quantified in this way. And if Sept. 11 does not reasonably generate new "requirements," nothing does.

Some in Congress have also grumbled about the tanker-lease innovation. Even some lawmakers who have strongly supported rebuilding America's defenses take a narrow and disparaging view of the Air Force's proposal. Maybe they have—but have not yet revealed—a better way to meet the urgent need for extending the effective range of the Air Force that protects us.

We would be wise to invest more in long-range bombers—more B-2s, for example—since the ability to operate globally on short notice will be vital to winning the war on terror. In the meantime, however, let's make the most of the fleet we have by supporting it properly.

**Messrs. Donnelly and Perle are resident fellows at the American Enterprise Institute.**

# Appendix E: Adbusters

## Why won't anyone say they are Jewish?

Friends help each other out. That's why the US sends billions of dollars every year to Israel. In return, Israel advances US strategic interests in the Middle East. But despite this mutual back scratching, Israeli-American relations are enduring a rough patch. Last December, a senior State Department official blasted Israel for having "done too little for far too long" to resolve the conflict with its Palestinian neighbors. Indeed, President Bush himself had scolded Israel a month earlier with his demand that "Israel should freeze settlement construction, dismantle unauthorized outposts, end the daily humiliation of the Palestinian people and not prejudice final negotiations with the building of walls and fences."

Harsh words, but is it all just window-dressing? This was not the first time Bush criticized Israel and he has made numerous calls for a "viable" Palestinian state during his presidency. Nevertheless, he has never concretely punished Israeli Prime Minister Ariel Sharon for ignoring US directives and shrugging off his commitment to the peace process. It's also worth noting that diplomatic admonitions are the responsibility of the State Department which has been on the losing end of the policy wars in Bush's White House. One wonders what Israeli-American relations, and indeed what American relations with the rest of the world would look like if the neocon hawks who control Rumsfeld's Defense Department were also in charge at State.

A lot of ink has been spilled chronicling the pro-Israel leanings of American neocons and fact that a the disproportionate percentage of them are Jewish. Some commentators are worried that these individuals – labeled 'Likudniks' for their

NORMAN PODHORETZ
IRVING KRISTOL
MIDGE DECTER
JEANE KIRKPATRICK
PAUL WOLFOWITZ
DOUGLAS FEITH
PETER RODMAN
STEPHEN CAMBONE
DONALD RUMSFELD
DICK CHENEY
I. LEWIS LIBBY
ELLIOT ABRAMS
ZALMAY KHALILZAD
JOHN BOLTON
DOV ZAKHEIM
ROBERT B. ZOELLICK
RICHARD PERLE
R. JAMES WOOLSEY
ELIOT COHEN
ROBERT W. TUCKER
FRANCIS FUKUYAMA
WILLIAM KRISTOL
ROBERT KAGAN
GARY SCHMITT
ELLEN BORK
DAVID WURMSER
JOSHUA MURAVCHIK
REUEL MARC GERECHT
MICHAEL NOVAK
FR. RICHARD J. NEUHAUS
MEYRAV WURMSER
IRWIN STELZER
RUPERT MURDOCH
RICHARD MELLON SCAIFE
THOMAS DONNELLY
OWEN HARRIES
MICHAEL LEDEEN
FRANK GAFFNEY
MAX BOOT
GARY BAUER
WILLIAM BENNETT
DANIEL PIPES
LAWRENCE KAPLAN
MARTY PERETZ
CHARLES KRAUTHAMMER
DAVID BROOKS
FRED BARNES
JOHN PODHORETZ
NEAL KOZODOY
JONAH GOLDBERG

## Deadly Dogma:
### How Neoconservatives Broke the Law to Deceive America

links to Israel's right wing Likud party – do not distinguish enough between American and Israeli interests. For example, whose interests were they protecting in pushing for war in Iraq?

Drawing attention to the Jewishness of the neocons is a tricky game. Anyone who does so can count on automatically being smeared as an anti-Semite. But the point is not that Jews (who make up less than 2 percent of the American population) have a monolithic perspective. Indeed, American Jews overwhelmingly vote Democrat and many of them disagree strongly with Ariel Sharon's policies and Bush's aggression in Iraq. The point is simply that the neocons seem to have a special affinity for Israel that influences their political thinking and consequently American foreign policy in the Middle East.

Here at Adbusters, we decided to tackle the issue head on and came up with a carefully researched list of who appear to be the 50 most influential neocons in the US (see above). Deciding exactly who is a neocon is difficult since some neocons reject the term while others embrace it. Some shape policy from within the White House, while others are more peripheral, exacting influence indirectly as journalists, academics and think tank policy wonks. What they all share is the view that the US is a benevolent hyper power that must protect itself by reshaping the rest of the world into its morally superior image. And half of the them are Jewish.

- Kalle Lasn

# End Notes

[1] "Mortality before and after the 2003 invasion of Iraq: cluster sample survey," Roberts, L., Lafta, R., Garfield, R., Khudhairi, J., Burnham, G., The Lancet - Vol. 364, Iss. 9448, 11/20/2004, pp. 1857-1864

[2] "Day 1,057 of the Iraq War," Pasadena Weekly, 4/14/2006, http://www.pasadenaweekly.com/article.php?id=2964&IssueNum=6

[3] "War's Stunning Price Tag," Dr. Stiglitz & Linda Bilmes, LA Times, January 17, 2006

[4] Introduction, The Neocon Reader, Irwin Selzter, Grove Press, 2004

[5] "Neocons are Wilsonian Idealists," Irwin Selzter, Introduction, The Neocon Reader, Grove Press, 2004

[6] National Security Strategy, p. 15

[7] "Neocons: The Men behind the Curtain," Khurram Husain. Bulletin of the Atomic Scientists, Chicago: Nov/Dec 2003. Vol. 59, Iss. 6, pp. 62-71

[8] Ibid.

[9] "Estimated Russian Stockpile, September 1996," Robert S. Norris & William M. Arkin, Bulletin of Atomic Scientists, September/October 1996, pp. 62-63 http://www.thebulletin.org/article_nn.php?art_ofn=so96norris

[10] Ibid.

[11] PNAC Open Letter to President Clinton, 11/26/1998

[12] "War Behind Closed Doors," Frontline, PBS, http://www.pbs.org/wgbh/pages/frontline/shows/iraq/

[13] "Baghdad Delenda Est, Part Two, Get On with It," Jonah Goldberg, National Review, 4/23/2002

[14] "A Hot War Led to a Cold Peace in the Mideast," Michael Mandelbaum, Council on Foreign Relations Op-Ed, 6/25/2005 http://www.cfr.org/publication/4635/hot_war_led_to_a_cold_peace_in_the_mideast.html?breadcrumb=default

[15] "Mythologies of the Gaza Withdrawal and 1967 War," WWRL-AM New York Drive Time Dialogue with Armstrong

Williams and Sam Greenfield, 8/15/2005 Radio Interview
Transcript http://www.irmep.org/armstrong.htm

[16] Excerpt from United States Department of Defense News
Transcript
Comments by Secretary of Defense Donald H. Rumsfeld,
August 6, 2002

[17] "The Time Of The Burning Sun: Six Days of War, Twelve
Weeks of Hope," Michael Bernet, Chester and West, NY,
2004, p. 2

[18] Foreign Relations, 1964-1968, Volume XIX, Arab-Israeli
Crisis and War, 1967,
http://www.state.gov/r/pa/ho/frus/johnsonlb/xix/28057.htm

[19] Ibid.

[20] Ibid.

[21] Ibid.

[22] "The 1967 War Revisited: New Sources and their
Implications," Speech, Charles Smith, University of Arizona
Near Eastern Studies Professor, U.S. State Department,
1/12/2004,
rtsp://cspanrm.fplive.net/cspan/archive/iraq/iraq011204_stated
ept.rm

[23] "Dying to Win: The Strategic Logic of Suicide Terrorism,"
Robert Pape, University of Chicago

[24] "White House Transcript of Bush-Sharon press conference
regarding Sharon's Gaza 'Disengagement' plan," April 14,
2004,
"http://electronicintifada.net/bytopic/historicalspeeches/262.sh
tml

[25] "The 1967 War Revisited: New Sources and their
Implications," Speech, Charles Smith, University of Arizona
Near Eastern Studies Professor, U.S. State Department,
1/12/2004,
rtsp://cspanrm.fplive.net/cspan/archive/iraq/iraq011204_stated
ept.rm

[26] "Iraq errors show West must act fast on Iran: Perle,"
Reuters, Feb 4, 2006

[27] "US 'reclassifying' public files," BBC, 2/21/2006, http://news.bbc.co.uk/2/hi/americas/4735570.stm

[28] "Olmert: Maale Adumim part of Israel," Ronny Sofer, Yedioth Ahronoth, 2/7/2006

[29] "A Clean Break: A New Strategy for Securing the Realm," Institute for Advanced Strategic and Political Studies

[30] "Rebuilding America's Defenses," p. 6.

[31] "Rebuilding America's Defenses," p. 6.

[32] "Rebuilding America's Defenses," p. 6.

[33] "Rebuilding America's Defenses," p. V.

[34] "Rebuilding America's Defenses," p. V.

[35] "Doppler Effect, Bow Waves, Shock Waves," http://online.cctt.org/physicslab/content/Phy1/lessonnotes/wav es/lessondoppler.asp

[36] "Ice-cold warrior," Peter H. Stone, National Journal Washington, Dec 23, 1995, Vol. 27, Iss. 51-52, p. 3146

[37] Ibid.

[38] Ibid.

[39] "The death of illusion," Frank Gaffney, Townhall.com, Sep 18, 2001, http://www.townhall.com/opinion/columns/frankjgaffneyjr/20 01/09/18/160665.html

[40] Wikipedia definition, http://en.wikipedia.org/wiki/Protection_racket

[41] "Pentagon report indicates Boeing investigations have widened," Joseph L. Galloway & Alan Bjerga, Knight Ridder, 3/31/2004

[42] "Pentagon finalizes Boeing tanker deal: Accord keeps alive Everett's 767 line," Charles Pope Seattle Post-Intelligencer Washington Correspondent, 11/7/2003

[43] "The Air Force's new lease on life," Frank Gaffney, Townhall.com, 9/3/2003

[44] "Richard Perle Libel Watch, Week 34," Slate Magazine, 11/14/2003, http://www.slate.com/id/2091198/

[45] "Gas Stations in the Sky," Richard Perle and Thomas Donnelly, Wall Street Journal, 8/14/2003

[46] "Newspaper Investigation Reveals Irregularities in Tanker Bid," Aero-News Network, 3/30/04, http://www.aero-

news.net/news/military.cfm?ContentBlockID=7200e5cb-bc1e-4013-b495-e55d837f6410&Dynamic=1

[47] "Pentagon report indicates Boeing investigations have widened," Joseph L. Galloway & Alan Bjerga, Knight Ridder, 3/31/2004

[48] "Newspaper Investigation Reveals Irregularities in Tanker Bid," Aero-News Network, 3/30/04, http://www.aero-news.net/news/military.cfm?ContentBlockID=7200e5cb-bc1e-4013-b495-e55d837f6410&Dynamic=1

[49] "Material withheld from Boeing tanker report angers Senate panel," Alicia Mundy, Seattle Times Washington bureau, 6/8/2005

[50] "Bush pushes to increase defense spending: Jump of 7% would top rest of world's military budgets," Eric Rosenberg, Hearst Newspapers, 2/12/2006 http://www.sfgate.com/cgi-bin/article.cgi?f=/c/a/2006/02/12/MNG41H78RK1.DTL

[51] "Transforming the Military Industrial Complex," Speech by CEO Ron Sugar, Northrop Grumman, 10/10/2003. Transcript: http://www.irmep.org/8_10_2003_AEI_Future_of_Defense.html

[52] CNN Interview, Wolf Blitzer, September 8, 2002

[53] Wolfowitz Interview with Sam Tannenhaus, Vanity Fair, 5/30/2003

[54] "The Downing Street Memo," classified UK gov't document, Matthew Rycroft, 7/23/2002, http://www.timesonline.co.uk/article/0,,2087-1593607,00.html

[55] National Review Online, August 6, 2002

[56] http://zfacts.com/p/130.html

[57] "Rebuilding America's Defenses"

[58] "Artificial Intelligence? Now" with David Broncaccio, PBS, http://www.pbs.org/now/archive_transcripts.html, 2/3/2006

[59] "Definition of Hoax," Merriam-Webster Online, http://www.m-w.com/dictionary/hoax

[60] "Ex-CIA Official Faults Use of Data on Iraq," Walter Pincus, Washington Post, 2/10/2006

[61] Wikipedia, http://en.wikipedia.org/wiki/Leo_Strauss

[62] The Republic, Plato, 360 BCE

[63] "Misperceptions, the Media and the Iraq War," Principal Investigator Steven Kull, October 2, 2003, http://www.pipa.org/OnlineReports/Iraq/IraqMedia_Oct03/Ira qMedia_Oct03_rpt.pdf

[64] Source: House Committee on Appropriations Hearing on a Supplemental War Regulation, 3/27/03

[65] "War's Stunning Price Tag," Dr. Stiglitz & Linda Bilmes, LA Times, January 17, 2006

[66] "Crude Designs, The Rip-Off of Iraq's Oil Wealth," Gregg Muitt, November 2005, http://www.globalpolicy.org/security/oil/2005/crudedesigns.ht m

[67] Editorial, William Kristol, The Weekly Standard, Washington, Nov 21, 2005. Vol. 11, Iss. 10, p. 9

[68] Source: Gallup / CNN / USA Today - Methodology: Telephone interviews with 1,006 American adults, conducted from Jan. 20 to Jan. 22, 2006. Margin of error is 3 percent. http://IRmep.org/datafile.htm

[69] NSA declassified documents released on 11/30/05, http://www.nsa.gov/vietnam/index.cfm

[70] "Tonkin Gulf reports cooked? Historian's research finds intelligence errors covered up," Scott Shane, New York Times, 10/31/2005

[71] "Davos Chair apologizes for magazine's Israel boycott call," Haaretz, 1/26/2006

[72] http://www.editorandpublisher.com/editorandpublisher/headli nes/article_display.jsp?vnu_content_id=204451

[73] Interview with David Radler, Maclean's Magazine, 2/3/92

[74] "Standing Up for Israel," F. David Radler, Chicago Sun-Times, 10/13/2002, http://www.aish.com/SSI/articleToPrint.asp?PageURL=/jewis hissues/mediaobjectivity/Standing_Up_for_Israel.xml&torahp ortion=

[75] "SEC sues 2 ousted Hollinger executives: Regulators allege Black, Radler cheated investors," James P. Miller, Chicago Tribune, 11/16/2004,

http://www.chicagotribune.com/business/chi-0411160266nov16,1,6883287.story?coll=chi-business-hed
[76] What's in missing black boxes? U.S. judge in probe issues subpoena wants documents from 10 Toronto St.," Rick Westhead, Chicago Tribune, 2/8/2006.
[77] "Ex-Hollinger official: Give me my stuff back," Eric Herman, Chicago Sun-Times, 2/11/2006
[78] "Are George Will's conflicts none of your business?" 1/9/2004, http://www.fair.org/activism/will-disclosure.html
[79] "Hollinger Reveals Details of Suit," David S. Hilzenrath, Washington Post, 11/2/2004
[80] "Rupert Murdoch's Televised Views on Israel," Fifteen Minutes magazine, Issue 35, April 2002
[81] "Ice-cold warrior," Peter H. Stone, National Journal Washington, Dec 23, 1995. Vol. 27, Iss. 51-52, p. 3146
[82] Ibid.
[83] Exclusive Interview with Condoleeza Rice, The Jewish Press, 5/13/2003
[84] "Douglas Feith, Portrait of a Neoconservative," Tom Barry, Antiwar.com, 9/15/2004
http://www.antiwar.com/barry/?articleid=3545
[85] Feith and Zell website, www.fandz.com
[86] Letters to the Editor, Washington Post, Sept 16, 2004
[87] "What Bush Isn't Saying About Iraq: President Bush won't discuss two big reasons he wants to invade Iraq," Michael Kinsley, Slate magazine, 10/24/2002
http://www.slate.com/id/2073093
[88] Adbusters, March/April 2004,
http://canadiancoalition.com/adbusters01/
[89] "For Vietnam Vet Anthony Zinni, Another War on Shaky Territory," Thomas E. Ricks, Washington Post, 12/23/2003
[90] "General Zinni, what a Ninny," Joel Mowbray, Townhall.com, 12/31/2003
http://www.townhall.com/opinion/columns/joelmowbray/2003/12/31/160652.html
[91] "Definition of Militant," Merriam-Webster Online, http://www.m-w.com/dictionary/militant

[92] "Scars of War, Wounds of Peace: The Israeli-Arab Tragedy," Shlomo Ben-Ami, Oxford University Press, February 1, 2006

[93] Ibid.

[94] Shields and Brooks, The NewsHour with Jim Lehrer, 1/27/2006, http://www.pbs.org/newshour/bb/political_wrap/jan-june06/sb_1-27.html

[95] About Lehi Group, http://experts.about.com/e/l/le/Lehi_(group).htm

[96] Winston Churchill, confidential notes, July 2, 1943

[97] "Neocon Middle East Policy: The 'Clean Break' Plan Damage Assessment," IRmep Publishing, 2005, p. 62

[98] "Farewell Address," George Washington, 9/19/1796 http://usinfo.state.gov/usa/infousa/facts/democrac/49.htm

[99] "An End to Evil," Interview with Author Richard Perle, Book Notes, 3/7/2004

[100] "Where the Right Went Wrong: How Neoconservatives Subverted the Reagan Revolution and Hijacked the Bush Presidency," Patrick J. Buchanan, Thomas Dunne Books, 2004, p. 28

[101] "War critics astonished as US hawk admits invasion was illegal," The Guardian, 11/20/2003, http://www.guardian.co.uk/Iraq/Story/0,2763,1089158,00.html

[102] "The Limits of International Law," 3/30/2005, http://www.aei.org/events/filter.all,eventID.1023/transcript.asp

[103] "The Global Prosecutors," John Bolton, American Enterprise Institute, http://www.aei.org/publications/pubID.17515,filter.all/pub_detail.asp

[104] "The Limits of International Law," 3/30/2005, http://www.aei.org/events/filter.all,eventID.1023/transcript.asp

[105] "Will the 'World's Greatest Deliberative Body' Deliberate About the Flawed Start II Treaty?" Frank Gaffney, Center for Security Policy, 12/11/1995,

http://www.centerforsecuritypolicy.org/index.jsp?section=pap
ers&code=95-D_103

[106] "Lunch with the Chairman: Why Was Richard Perle
meeting with Adnan Khashoggi?" Seymour Hersh, The New
Yorker, 3/10/2003

[107] Ibid.

[108] Ibid.

[109] "Seizing Arab Oil," Miles Ignotus, Harper's Magazine,
March 1975, http://www.harpers.org/SeizingArabOil.html

[110] "Lunch with the Chairman: Why Was Richard Perle
meeting with Adnan Khashoggi?" Seymour Hersh, The New
Yorker, 3/10/2003

[111] IRS Form 990 Filing, New Citizenship Project

[112] Source: PNAC website,
http://www.newamericancentury.org/

[113] IRS Form 990 Filing, New Citizenship Project

[114]"No one knows full cost of Israel's settlement ambitions,"
USA Today, 8/14/2005,
http://www.usatoday.com/news/world/2005-08-14-
israelsettlercosts_x.htm

[115] "Summary of the Opinion Concerning Unauthorized
Outposts," Talia Sasson, 3/10/2005,
http://domino.un.org/UNISPAL.NSF/0/956aa60f2a7bd6a1852
56fc0006305f4?OpenDocument

[116]"Dying to Win: The Strategic Logic of Suicide Terrorism,"
Robert Pape, http://www.amazon.com/exec/obidos/tg/detail/-
/1400063175/103-1676732-6156641?v=glance

[117]"How many filings, how much revenue?" All Things
Considered, National Public Radio, November 12, 2004.

[118]"Senatorial Courtesy," Lou Dubose, Texas Observer,
8/26/2005,
http://www.texasobserver.org/showArticle.asp?ArticleID=201
6

[119]"Ten Things Every American Can Do to Improve US
Middle East Policy," Web Presentation,
http://www.irmep.org/terrorism.htm

[120] "Jewish Officials Profess Shock Over Report on Zionist Body," Forward, 3/18/2005, http://www.jafi.org.il/papers/2005/march/march18afor.htm

[121] "The 9/11 Commission Report," p. 147, http://www.gpoaccess.gov/911/

[122] "Norman Finkelstein & Former Israeli Foreign Minister Shlomo Ben-Ami Debate: Complete Transcript," Democracy Now radio broadcast, 2/14/2006, http://www.democracynow.org/finkelstein-benami.shtml

[123] "Election Panel Can Be Sued," Richard Carelli, 6/1/1998, http://www.washingtonpost.com/wp-srv/national/longterm/supcourt/stories/ap060198.htm

[124] "Jail sentence mutes freedom's ring," Gary Wasserman, Washington Post Op-Ed, 2/20/2006, http://www.timesunion.com/AspStories/story.asp?storyID=452646&category=OPINION&newsdate=2/20/2006&TextPage=2

[125] Legal Brief, United States v. Franklin, Defense Counsel: John Nassikas III, Arent Fox, Washington, D.C.; Abbe Lowell, Chadbourne & Parke, Washington, D.C.

[126] "Serving Two Flags: Neocons, Israel and the Bush Administration," Stephen Green, May 2004

[127] Ibid.

[128] Ibid.

[129] Ibid.

[130] "US acts over Israeli arms sales to China," Conal Urquhart, The Guardian, 6/13/2003, http://www.guardian.co.uk/israel/Story/0,,1505209,00.html

[131] "Pentagon investigation of Iraq war hawk stalling Senate inquiry into pre-war Iraq intelligence," Larisa Alexandrovna, Raw Story, 1/30/2006

[132] Ibid.

[133] "Open Door Policy," Karen Kwiatkowski, The American Conservative, 1/15/2004, http://www.amconmag.com/2004_01_19/article1.html

[134] "American who advised Pentagon says he wrote for magazine that found forged Niger documents," Larisa Alexandrovna, Raw Story, 1/17/2006,

http://rawstory.com/news/2005/American_who_consulted_for_Pentagon_says_0117.html

[135]"Perspectives on Pollard," Michael Saba, http://www.mediamonitors.net/saba1.html

[136] "Dismiss AIPAC Charges, Duo Asks," Jerry Seper, Washington Times, 2/16/2006, http://washingtontimes.com/national/20060215-113838-3636r.htm

[137] Interview with Gen. Wesley Clark, NBC's Meet the Press, 6/15/2003

[138] "Israel After Sharon," Meyrav Wurmser Presentation, Hudson Institute, 1/9/2006, http://www.hudson.org/index.cfm?fuseaction=hudson_upcoming_events&id=228

[139] "Aide Urged Pentagon to Consider Weapons Made by Former Client," Jeff Gerth, New York Times, April 17, 1983

[140] "Perle: 'Prince of Darkness' in the spotlight," Jim Lobe, Asia Times, 3/25/2003

[141] "Nine Professors at Columbia Are Deemed 'Dangerous,'" Alec Magnet, New York Sun, 2/21/2006

Printed in the United States
201753BV00001B/19-27/A

9 780976 443742